The Behavior of Financial Markets under Rational Expectations

HAN Yan

Bridge21 | Alhambra, CA

The Behavior of Financial Markets under Rational Expectations
By HAN Yan

Published by Bridge21 Publications, LLC

Distributed by Casemate Group
Casemate Academic (Havertown, Pennsylvania): USA and North America
Oxbow Books (Oxford): UK, Europe, and the Rest of the World

This research was sponsored by the National Natural Science Foundation of China under grant number 71772013.

Published in the United States of America

ISBN 978-1-62643-087-7 Hardcover
ISBN 978-1-62643-088-4 ePub | ebook pdf | Kindle

Contents

Chapter 1 Information **1**
1.1 Rational expectations 1
1.2 Different opinions 3
1.3 Information aggregation and learning 4
1.3.1 Information percolation and learning 4
1.3.2 Hidden information 6
1.3.3 Price informativeness 7
1.4 How do agents learn new information 7
1.5 Information and pricing 8
1.5.1 Information asymmetry and asset pricing 8
1.5.2 Liquidity and asset pricing 9
1.6 Further issues of learning and reacting 11
1.7 Information providers 11

Chapter 2 How are prices formed? **13**
2.1 The perspective of asset pricing literature 13
2.2 Inventory costs based microstructure models 14
2.3 Information based microstructure models 15
2.4 What is risk? 18
2.5 Trading mechanism 19
2.6 Short selling 20
2.7 Other topics in microstructure 20

Chapter 3 Liquidity **22**
3.1 Measuring liquidity 22
3.2 Volume 24
3.3 Determinants of liquidity 26
3.4 Markets' and liquidity providers' conditions and liquidity 27
3.5 The effect of liquidity on the firm's well-being 28
3.6 Who is providing liquidity 28

Chapter 4 Limit orders **30**
4.1 The models of limit orders 30
4.2 Investor's choice of limit versus market orders 33
4.3 Limit order revisions and aggressiveness 35
4.4 Limit order patterns 36

Chapter 5 Depicting investors **38**
5.1 Theory based investor taxonomy 38
5.1.1 Informed investors 39
5.1.2 Liquidity investors, noise investors, and speculators 39
5.2 Identity based investor taxonomy 41
5.2.1 Individual investors 41
5.2.2 Institutional investors 42
5.2.3 Foreign investors 43
5.3 Investor sophistication 44
5.3.1 What does sophistication mean? 44
5.3.2 The effect of investor sophistication 44
5.4 Herding and correlated trading 45
5.4.1 Empirical evidence 45
5.4.2 Theoretical explanations 45
5.5 Trading behavior 47
5.5.1 Trading and contemporaneous returns 47
5.5.2 Trading horizon 48
5.5.3 Value investing 48

Chapter 6 Mutual funds **50**
6.1 Fund performance and fund manager skills 50
6.1.1 Overview of fund manager skills 50
6.1.2 Factors affecting fund performance 51

6.2 Funds herding 52
6.3 Incentives and the risk shifting 53
6.4 Fund flow and investor's preferences 54
6.4.1 Flow-performance relationship 54
6.4.2 Explanations for asymmetric performance-flow relationship 55
6.4.3 Investor's purchasing process 55
6.4.4 Advertising 56
6.4.5 Smart or dumb money effect 56
6.5 Fund fees 57
6.6 Governance of funds 58

Chapter 7 Prices of IPO and SEO 60
7.1 Why and when to issue new equities 60
7.2 Choice of issue types 62
7.3 New issuance pricing 63
7.4 Trading around IPO and SEO 63
7.5 Market reaction and long term performance 64

Chapter 8 Behavioral explanation 67
8.1 General discussion on the behavioral explanation 67
8.2 Disposition effect and prospect theory 68
8.3 Overconfidence and over-reaction 69
8.4 Awareness, familiarity, and attention 70
8.5 Law of small numbers 71
8.6 Rational structural uncertainty models 72

Chapter 9 Modeling economic behavior 74
9.1 Nash equilibrium 74
9.1.1 Dominant and dominated strategy 74
9.1.2 Definition of Nash equilibrium 76
9.1.3 Evolutionary stability 77
9.1.4 Continuous strategy space 78
9.2 Bayesian games 79
9.3 Utility maximization models 82

Chapter 10 Mathematical techniques for economic modeling 83

10.1 Difference equations 84
10.2 Differential equations 84
10.2.1 Existence and uniqueness of the solutions 84
10.2.2 Solving one-variable first-order differential equation 85
10.2.3 General method solving high order linear differential equations 86
10.3 Fixed point 88
10.4 Static optimization 90
10.5 Duality 91

Chapter 11 Empirical methodology 93

11.1 Regressions 93
11.1.1 Simple regressions 93
11.1.2 Regression discontinuity 94
11.1.3 Ordered probit regression 94
11.1.4 Vector autoregression 95
11.1.5 Panel data regressions 96
11.2 Non-regression methods 98
11.3 Endogeneity 101
11.3.1 Natural experiment 102
11.3.2 Difference approach 103
11.3.3 Instrumental variables 103
11.3.4 Simultaneous equations 103
11.3.5 Self-selection and Heckman model 104
11.3.6 Smart experimental designs getting around endogeneity 104
11.3.7 When should we be concerned about endogeneity 105
11.3.8 Other research design issues 105
11.4 Measurements 106
11.4.1 Sample and data 106
11.4.2 Information and risk 107
11.4.3 Trading 108
11.4.4 Firm characteristics 109
11.4.5 Asset pricing related measures 109

Bibliography 111

Chapter 1
Information

1.1 Rational expectations

Rational expectation models are arguably the most important starting point for understanding the economic behaviors in financial markets. The notable seminal works along this line of research are: Milgrom (1981), Grossman (1981), and Milgrom and Stokey (1982).

Hellwig (1980, p. 479) shows that for an agent with constant absolute risk aversion (CARA), her demand for the risky asset is independent of her initial wealth. Admati (1985) extends Hellwig (1980) into multi assets. The following is from Admati (1985) except for some change in notation.

There is a continuum of agents, indexed by i, in the interval $[0,1]$.[1] They trade in two periods. In period 0, each agent allocates her initial wealth w_{0i} between one riskless asset, and n risky assets. Let $\mathbf{p}$ be the price vector of the risky assets.[2] In period 1, the riskless asset pays r units, and the risky assets pay $\mathbf{v}$ units of the single consumption good. Therefore the terminal wealth for agent i is given by

$$\widetilde{w}_{1i} = w_{0i}r + \mathbf{x}_i^T(\mathbf{v} - r\mathbf{p}) \tag{1.1}$$

1 This continuum assumption has several nice properties. We actually assume infinite number of agents in the economy. Hence it is reasonable to view every agent as a price taker.

2 Price vector $\mathbf{p}$ does not contain the price for the riskless asset, as we take the riskless asset to be the numeraire.

where $\mathbf{x}_i$ is agent *i*'s optimal holding of the risky assets, which maximizes her expected utility $u_i(\widetilde{w}_1) =- e^{(-\widetilde{w}_1/\gamma_i)}$.

Further suppose before allocating her wealth in period 0, agent *i* receives a private signal $\mathbf{s}_i$ concerning about **v**, i.e., $\mathbf{s}_i = \mathbf{v} + \boldsymbol{\varepsilon}_i$. And there is a per capita random supply shock **z** for the risky assets. Let **V**, **U**, and $\mathbf{S}_i$ be the variance-covariance matrices of **v**, **z**, and $\boldsymbol{\varepsilon}_i$.

The equilibrium satisfies the following conditions:

1. Optimal holding condition: $\mathbf{x}_i(\mathbf{s}_i, \mathbf{p}) \in \operatorname{argmax}_{\mathbf{x}_i} \mathbb{E}\big(u_i(w_{1i}|\mathbf{s}_i, \mathbf{p})\big)$.
2. Market clearing condition: $\int_0^1 x_i\,(\mathbf{s}_i, \mathbf{p})\, di = \mathbf{z}$. .

Admati (1985, p. 637) shows that there is a unique linear equilibrium price function of the form

$$\mathbf{p} = \mathbf{a}_0 + \mathbf{A}_1\mathbf{v} - \mathbf{A}_2\mathbf{z} \tag{1.2}$$

$$\mathbf{a}_0 = \frac{\gamma}{r}(\gamma\mathbf{V}^{-1} + \gamma\mathbf{QU}^{-1}\mathbf{Q} + \mathbf{Q})^{-1}(\mathbf{V}^{-1}\bar{\mathbf{v}} + \mathbf{QU}^{-1}\bar{\mathbf{z}}) \tag{1.3}$$

$$\mathbf{A}_1 = \frac{1}{r}(\gamma\mathbf{V}^{-1} + \gamma\mathbf{QU}^{-1}\mathbf{Q} + \mathbf{Q})^{-1}(\mathbf{Q} + \gamma\mathbf{QU}^{-1}\mathbf{Q}) \tag{1.4}$$

$$\mathbf{A}_2 = \frac{1}{r}(\gamma\mathbf{V}^{-1} + \gamma\mathbf{QU}^{-1}\mathbf{Q} + \mathbf{Q})^{-1}(\mathbf{I} + \gamma\mathbf{QU}^{-1}) \tag{1.5}$$

where $\gamma = \int_0^1 \gamma_i \, di$ and $\mathbf{Q} = \int_0^1 \gamma_i \, \mathbf{S}_i^{-1} \, di.$.

Agent *i*'s conditional expectation of **v** is given by (Admati 1985, p. 639)

$$\mathbb{E}(\mathbf{v}|\mathbf{s}_i, \mathbf{p}) = \mathbf{b}_{0i} + \mathbf{B}_{1i}\mathbf{s}_i + \mathbf{B}_{2i}\mathbf{p} \tag{1.6}$$

$$\mathbf{b}_{0i} = \mathbf{V}_i\big[\mathbf{I} - (\mathbf{UQ}^{-1} + \gamma\mathbf{I})^{-1}\big](\mathbf{V}^{-1}\bar{\mathbf{v}} + \mathbf{QU}^{-1}\bar{\mathbf{z}}) \tag{1.7}$$

$$\mathbf{B}_{1i} = \mathbf{V}_i\mathbf{S}_i^{-1} = \big[\mathbf{S}_i(\mathbf{V}^{-1} + \mathbf{QU}^{-1}) + \mathbf{I}\big]^{-1} \tag{1.8}$$

$$\mathbf{B}_{2i} = r\mathbf{V}_i\mathbf{QU}^{-1}\mathbf{A}_2^{-1} \tag{1.9}$$

where $\mathbf{V}_i = \mathbb{V}\text{ar}(\mathbf{v}|\mathbf{s}_i, \mathbf{p})$ is not necessarily equal to the unconditional variance covariance matrix **V**.

And the equilibrium demand function of agent *i* is given by (Admati, 1985, pp. 639–640):

$$
\begin{aligned}
\mathbf{x}_i(\mathbf{s}_i, \mathbf{p}) &= \mathbf{g}_{0i} + \mathbf{G}_{1i}\mathbf{s}_i - \mathbf{G}_{2i}\mathbf{p} && (1.10)\\
\mathbf{g}_{0i} &= \gamma_i\left[\mathbf{I} - (\mathbf{UQ}^{-1} + \gamma\mathbf{I})^{-1}\right](\mathbf{V}^{-1}\mathbf{v} + \mathbf{QU}^{-1}\bar{\mathbf{z}}) && (1.11)\\
\mathbf{G}_{1i} &= \gamma_i\mathbf{S}_i^{-1} && (1.12)\\
\mathbf{G}_{2i} &= \gamma_i\left(\mathbf{A}_2^{-1} - r\gamma\mathbf{Q} + r\mathbf{S}_i^{-1}\right) && (1.13)
\end{aligned}
$$

1.2 Different opinions

It should be noted that rational expectation models assume that agents have heterogeneous beliefs. This forms an important distinct from **representative agent paradigm** in the "traditional economic models." The traditional economic models typically assume that there is a **representative agent**, which represent all the agents (investors) in the game. By assuming a representative agent, the traditional economic models implicitly assume that all agents (investors) share the same belief, i.e., homogeneous beliefs. Although one can argue that the distinction between heterogeneous versus homogeneous beliefs is nothing more than different modeling techniques, with this distinction becoming vital for understanding the economic behaviors in financial markets, because the dynamics of financial markets are essentially driven by the interactions among investors who hold different beliefs. Put differently, a market in which all investors share the same belief is a "dead" market because no one has the incentive to buy or sell the financial instruments. That is why we shall pay close attentions to the models' aspects of **different opinions.**

Lamont (2012, p. 5) provides an excellent explanation for different opinions:

Harrison and Kreps (1978) construct a model with rational investors where differences of opinion, together with short sale constraints, create a "speculative premium" in which stock prices are higher than even the most optimistic investor's assessment of their value (see also Duffie, Garleanu, and Pedersen 2002). These differences of opinion can be interpreted as arising from different prior beliefs, which rationally converge as information arrives (Morris, 1996), or as irrational overconfidence (Scheinkman and Xiong, 2003).

A key feature of rational expectation model is that investors are trying to infer other investors' private information, and update their information according to the inference. If we assume investors "agree to disagree," or put it alternatively, investors hold dogmatic belief, that is, they simply deem wrong what the others believe. There's a term, "agree to disagree," to summarize this situation.[3]

Diether et al. (2002) use the analyst dispersion to proxy divergence of opinion, and find that higher divergence of opinion is followed by a lower future stock return. Chen et al. (2002) use the mutual fund ownership as the divergence of opinion proxy, and find that higher divergence of opinion is associated with higher stock price. Chatterjee et al. (2012) argue that these two pieces of evidence support Miller's (1977) prediction that "the greater the divergence of opinion among investors about the security's value, the higher the security's market price."

Moeller et al. (2007) show that the higher diversity of opinion decreases the acquirer's return in stock payment acquisitions, with cash payment acquisitions unaffected.

Kim (2013) shows that there are pricing errors at the opening sessions, and the errors are more pronounced among the stocks that trade earlier. The evidence supports the idea that investors learn from each other and this learning process inevitably incurs errors, especially at its early stage.

1.3 Information aggregation and learning

1.3.1 Information percolation and learning

Some market indicators, among which is surely the stock price, serve as information aggregators. Stock price aggregate all the information on the market. This is the fundamental belief behind market efficiency. The inquiry on information aggregation can be categorized into two lines. One line of research focuses on the equilibrium result of information aggregation, e.g., Grossman (1976). The other line of research focuses on the micro-level process of information aggregation, e.g., Kyle (1985). Besides stock price, trading volume is also viewed as containing information, e.g., Schneider (2009).

Why can these indicators serve as information aggregator? The most important reason is that every investor tries to infer other agent's private information by observing these indicators. It's this process that aggregates all the agent's private information. Rational expectation models depicts these processes.

3 See Milton and Raviv (1993), Kandel and Pearson (1995), Hong and Stein (1999), Daniel et al. (2001), Scheinkman and Xiong (2003), Morris (1996), and Odean (1998b) for further discussions on this topic

The competition among insiders drive stock price to its true value more quickly. See Holden and Subrahmanyam (1994, 1992), Foster and Viswanathan (1996), Back et al. (2000), and Baruch (2002).

In Kyle's (1985) model, information is gradually incorporated into price, because the informed trader with monopoly power splits her order. Baruch (2002), Back et al. (2000), Foster and Viswanathan (1996, 1994, 1993), Holden and Subrahmanyam (1994, 1992), and Admati and Pfleiderer (1988) extend Kyle's (1985) model, allowing for multiple informed traders.

A key role of market is to aggregate the private information held by various agents (Hayek, 1945). For this process to occur, agents must infer others information and update theirs. This inferring-updating process is also studied under terms like "information percolation" and "learning." Here learning means that investors interpret their own and infer other investors' signals. Another similar concept of learning is learning by doing. That is, investors improve their investment skills through the accumulation of experiences. Experiences, of course, can help investors better understand and use the signals. But it seems that the learning by doing literature emphasizes more on long term effect of the improved skills, rather than the signal interpretation in individual decisions. So in this subsection, the learning refers to the interpretation of signals.

Duffie et al. (2010) define two channels of information percolation. One is the public channel, and the other is the private channel: "Information aggregation occurs through the public observation of variables that reflect other agents' actions (such as prices or public bids for an asset) or through the private observation of other agents' actions (such as bilateral bargaining in a decentralized market). ... Private information sharing is typical in functioning over-the-counter markets for many types of financial assets, including bonds and derivatives. In these markets, trades occur at private meetings in which counterparties offer prices that reveal information to each other, but not to other market participants. In addition to this form of private information sharing, many over-the-counter markets also have public releases of a selection of price quotations or executed trades" (pp. 1575–1576). The main conclusion is summarized in the abstract: "[i]f the private learning channel is present, convergence of the distribution of beliefs to the perfect-information limit is exponential at a rate equal to the sum of the mean arrival rate of public information and the mean rate at which individual agents are randomly matched with other agents. If, however, there is no private information sharing, then convergence is exponential at a rate strictly lower than the mean arrival rate of public information."

Nicolosi et al. (2009, p. 318) make and prove the following argument:

> [I]nvestors' demand for risky assets will increase with their confidence in their private signal precision. Specially, if investors privately receive signals (e.g., ranging from negative one to positive one) regarding the quality of potential purchases' future returns, then investors who believe their signals to be perfectly accurate (based on their previous trades' subsequent returns) would be willing to trade whenever the signals were, even marginally, positive. However, if investors believe their signals to be less accurate, then they would be less willing to trade after receiving only slightly positive signals. Clearly, investors' willingness to trade would increase with their perceived signal precision.

Nicolosi et al. (2009) "provide strong evidence that [trading] ability measures significantly affect investors' future investment performance and trade intensity. [And] trading experience helps future investment performance."

It's now a too simple assumption that informed traders are just informed due to exogenous reasons. Whether or not to acquire costly information is a decision for a trader to make. Incorporating this endogenous information acquisition makes the model better. The following models assume endogenous information acquisition: Goettler et al. (2009), Mendelson and Tunca (2004).

1.3.2 Hidden information

Hong and Stein (2003) argue that short-sale-constrained investors have to sit out of the market when the market price is higher than their deemed value. Therefore, these investors' private information does not reflect the market price. Their private information becomes incorporated when the market price is low so that they can begin to buy the stock. This hidden information leads to changes in price, volatility, and volume even without new information coming to the market. Romer (1993) also discusses hidden information. But his hidden information is symmetric, whereas Hong and Stein's (2003) is asymmetric.

Chen et al. (2002) empirically test the idea of hidden information. They use the breadth of ownership as a proxy of the private information excluded from the market price. That is, if the stock ownership becomes concentrated in the hands of some investors, then more investors just sit out of the market if they cannot short sell. Therefore the contemporaneous price of concentrated owned stocks are inherently optimistic, because only the optimist's information is incorporated in the price. Hence the subsequent stock price will be lower, i.e., the following stock return is low. They refer to the hidden information as "pent-up" information.

1.3.3 Price informativeness

Price reflects information. My fundamental idea is that the only channel of price's incorporating information is informed trading. Consider the following players in this game: maker makers, informed and liquidity traders, analysts, intermediaries, affiliated investment banks[4] (Ellis et al., 2000; Schultz, 2003), etc.

Anand et al. (2011) argue that location is a factor that determines the incorporation of information into prices. Similar evidences include the papers cited in footnote 5 on p. 194. Also see Loughran and Schultz (2005).

1.4 How do agents learn new information

First, can agents learn? This is an important question, although it seems to have received little attention in the literature. Many models simply assume that eventually agents can learn the "truth." However, Blume and Easley (1982) and Bray and Savin (1986) show that learning does not necessarily lead agents to the true model.

Given that there is no guarantee that learning necessarily leads the agents to the truth, some researchers propose a notion called "reinforcement learning." Reinforcement learning refers to the situation in which past success makes investors more firmly hold their beliefs; see also Erev and Roth (1998), Charness and Levin (2005), Kaustia and Knüpfer (2008), and Malmendier and Nagel (2011). Choi et al. (2009) document that investors increase their 401(k) savings after experiencing "particularly rewarding outcomes from 401(k) saving—a high average and/or low variance return." Similar evidence is provided by Strahilevitz et al. (2011).

Another type of learning is that investors, especially individual investors, learn by doing. Seru et al. (2010) show that individual investors improve their investment ability over time by reducing the disposition effect, and some of them also cease to trade when they realize their low investment ability. The following

4 Investment banks include underwriters and M&A advisers.

studies support the view that investors improve their skills over time: Coursey et al. (1987), Dhar and Zhu (2006), Erev and Roth (1998), and List (2003) use experiments; Nicolosi et al. (2009) use empirical evidence. The following studies show that learning takes a long time: Knetsch and Sinden (1984) and Camerer and Hogarth (1999). Greenwood and Nagel (2009) study how U.S. mutual fund managers invested during the Internet bubble in the beginning of this century. They document that younger managers, presumably inexperienced relative to their old peers, tilted their portfolios toward Internet stocks during the bubble. Their evidence show that inexperience plays a role in determining how investors choose stocks.

1.5 Information and pricing

1.5.1 Information asymmetry and asset pricing

Easley and O'Hara (2004) provide a theoretical model, arguing that asymmetric information should be priced, because traders are less willing to hold stocks with more severe asymmetric information; thus these stocks command a premium. However, Hughes et al. (2007) and Lambert et al. (2007) argue that Easley and O'Hara (2004) obtain the result because the agents in their model hold under-diversified portfolios, although it should be noted that under-diversification may be the norm, and therefore the challenge by Hughes et al. (2007) and Lambert et al. (2007) may be irrelevant.

Lambert et al. (2012) develop a model similar to Kyle's (1985). The authors show that the information asymmetry per se has no effect in pricing as long as the market is completely competitive. What matters is the average information precision. However, when the market is not competitive, both information asymmetry and information precision are priced. The competitive market refers to the circumstance under which traders are price takers. In the spirit of Kyle's (1985), in a competitive market Kyle's (1985) λ equals 0. To understand Lambert et al.'s (2012) argument, notice that both Easley and O'Hara (2004) and Lambert et al. (2012) argue that information precision is the key for traders to hold the stock. Consider a stock haunted by severe asymmetric information. More informed trading makes the stock price more informative, thus compensating uninformed traders' informational disadvantage.

There are also arguments that asymmetric information does affect pricing, but toward an unclear direction. In Wang's (1993) model, asymmetric information has two effects. On the one hand, it reduces traders' willingness to hold an opaque stock, thus depressing the price. On the other hand, more informed trading makes the price more informative, thus uninformed traders should be less concerned about the asymmetric information problem. Christensen et al. (2010) argue that before the release of information, (asymmetric) information risk may command a risk premium. When the uncertainty is resolved upon the release of the information, there is a decrease in the (asymmetric) information risk. Therefore, when the cost of capital is measured in the long run, difference in the information environment does not lead to a risk premium.

Kelly and Ljungqvist (2012) show that when the analyst coverage is lower for a stock, the demand from uninformed investors is also lower. They interpret this evidence as supporting the idea that asymmetric information is a price factor. Similar to Easley and O'Hara's (2004) argument, accounting literature contends that accounting data quality is a pricing factor, because it affects the information precision of traders. See El Ghoul et al. (2013, footnote 3, pp. 141–142) for the review on this literature. Easley et al. (2002) show that PIN is positively related to future realized returns. However, Mohanram and Rajgopal (2009) show that PIN is not priced. Hwang et al. (2013) show that PIN, when purged of a liquidity component according to Duarte and Young's (2009) method, is priced.

1.5.2 Liquidity and asset pricing

Information asymmetry may be a pricing factor, because it affects traders' willingness to hold stocks, as argued by Easley and O'Hara (2004) and Lambert et al. (2012). There is another link in which information asymmetry may be priced: liquidity. Because of information asymmetry, there are bid and ask prices to compensate the information risk borne by market makers. That is the liquidity cost. So liquidity cost raises the cost of capital for the firm (Amihud and Mendelson, 1986a). In other words, liquidity is a pricing factor.

This line of research answers this question: is liquidity beta a risk factor to be priced? See the following papers: Pástor and Stambaugh (2003); Acharya and Pedersen (2005); Sadka (2006); Bekaert et al. (2007); Korajczyk and Sadka (2008); Brennan et al. (1998); Amihud (2002). See also Franzoni et al. (2012) and their footnote 1.

There are two lines on this topic. One line of research argues that illiquidity is a risk factor, because investors holding illiquid stocks may find it hard to find the counter party to trade the stocks. Let us call this view as *illiquidity risk*. This line of research finds expected returns are negatively related to various liquidity measures, for example the bid-ask spread by Amihud and Mendelson (1986b), price impact by Brennan and Subrahmanyam (1996), turnover by Datar et al. (1998), and trading volume by Brennan et al. (1998).

The other line of research deals with the individual stock's sensitivity to market wide liquidity. Let us call this view as *liquidity beta*, for example Pástor and Stambaugh (2003).

Can these two views be reconciled? Acharya and Pedersen (2005) and Korajczyk and Sadka (2008) provide evidences that both liquidity effects are priced. A surprising result found by Chordia, Subrahmanyam, and Anshuman (2001) shows that expected stock returns are negatively related to the volatility of liquidity. Pereira and Zhang (2010) provide an explanation for this anomaly. They assume the liquidity varies across time, and is mean-reversing. So higher volatility of liquidity provides investors with more opportunities to time their trading. Thus, the volatility is of option-like value, and investors demand lower expected return on these stocks.

Reinganum (1990) find that small firms have a smaller spread on NASDAQ than on NYSE. But this effect diminishes with increasing firm size. They argue the reason is that, for small firms, the benefit of multi dealership on NASDAQ outweighs the benefit of economy of scales enjoyed by sole dealership on NYSE. Bongaerts et al. (2011) propose a liquidity pricing model.

Brennan et al. (2012) estimate buy-order liquidity and sell-order liquidity separately using an adapted version of Glosten and Harris's (1988) model. The buy(sell)-order liquidity is an estimation of how much a market buy (sell) order moves the price. They show that sell-order liquidity is more strongly priced than buy-order liquidity.

As Acharya and Pedersen (2005) note, there are three lines of researches showing that liquidity is related to asset prices: liquidity beta is priced (Pástor and Stambaugh, 2003), average liquidity is priced (Amihud and Mendelson, 1986a), and liquidity comoves with and predicts returns (Bekaert et al. (2007); Chordia et al. (2005); Amihud (2002); Chordia, Roll, and Subrahmanyam (2001)). Acharya and Pedersen (2005) extend traditional CAPM model to incorporate liquidity costs. Their model shows four channels for liquidity costs to be priced (see eq. 8 on p. 381 and the discussions). Lee (2011) tests Acharya and Pedersen's (2005) model in global settings.

Although liquidity cost/risk is priced, it is unclear whether one component of liquidity cost, namely asymmetric information, is priced. Easley et al. (2002) discusses these papers on page 2187 of their text.

1.6 Further issues of learning and reacting

Bond et al. (2010) present an interesting angle to look at the price informativeness and the resulting actions. They argue that agents are likely to take actions when they observe a particular price: "Since market prices are forward looking, they reflect information not only about firms' fundamentals, but also about the resulting actions of various agents (i.e., directors, activists, regulators, or managers). In some cases, this considerably complicates the inference of information from the price. ... [L]earning from the price is complicated by the fact that two or more fundamentals may be associated with the same price" (p. 782). In other words, "the use of market data is self-defeating in the sense that the reflection of the expected market-based action in the price destroys the informational content of the price" (p. 783). An important implication of this study for the empirical research is that "if agents use the market price in their intervention decision, there will be dual causality between market prices and the intervention decision. ... Failing to account for the dual causality will produce results that appear as just a weak relation between prices and actions" (p. 784). For an example of accounting for this dual causality, see Bradley et al. (2010).

Another interesting issue is rumors and price manipulations. On the one hand, information on the market may not necessarily be true. On the other hand, rumors are not necessarily all false. van Bommel (2003) develops a model in which an informed trader with small and limited wealth may spread her private information to maximize her trading profit. The author also discusses other alike models (see p. 1501). In these models, a common question is whether the informed one bluffs (giving a signal when she has no private signal at all) or cheats (giving false signals). If informed traders do not send honest signals, they actually add noises to the market. And these models justify such behavior.

1.7 Information providers

Let us briefly review two groups of information providers: financial analysts and rating agencies.

Under the assumption that long term earnings forecast is less accurate than short term forecast, Da and Warachka (2011) argue that the disparity between long- and short-term forecasts is an ex ante proxy for errors in long term forecast. They further show that this disparity predicts future stock returns. They attribute this predictability to the failure of the analysts to incorporate information, which has been revealed by short term forecasts, into long term forecasts in a timely manner. And neither do the investors fully account for the information due to their limited attentions.

An important question is whether analysts' recommendations convey important information. A large number of studies have documented evidence that analysts' recommendations are an important information source. Altınkılıç et al. (2013) show that analysts forecast revisions have little information. These revisions simply follow significant events. Prior literature that employ multiday stock returns are not reliable since this measure is likely to overstate the informativeness of the analyst forecast revisions. However, other studies show that the IBES timestamps are not accurate, which leads to the insignificant returns around the analysts' recommendations.

He et al. (2012) show that conflicts of interests facing rating agencies distort the ratings. See the cited papers in this paper for more studies on rating agencies. Rating agencies are important because they provide important information about debt quality, and thus the cost of capital. Rating agencies are also blamed for their inflated ratings, which are deemed to be responsible for the recent financial crisis. This line of study also has implications on the banking system, as ratings have become an integral part of banking regulations.

Chapter 2
How are prices formed?

2.1 The perspective of asset pricing literature

There are several good papers reviewing the asset pricing literature from various perspectives, among which Cochrane (2011) is a good example. In a review by Nagel (2013), the author first provides a framework of the SDF factor model, then reviews the pricing factors, both "rational" and "irrational" ones. Notice that the author deems inaccurate the notions of rational/irrational and market efficiency. An important advancement in the asset pricing literature is to account for the return predictability. Additionally, investors need to take into account the parameter uncertainty. Bayesian portfolio allocations have attracted many attentions; see: Wachter (2010) and Avramov and Zhou (2010). On the methodology side, Lewellen et al. (2010) critique the traditional test methods and argue that the hurdle is too low to be met in claiming a new pricing factor. They propose four remedies to the potential problems of the traditional methods.

Researchers have documented the following stylized facts of returns.

1. Negative skewness. Stocks are prone to melt down rather than melt up (see Hong and Stein, 2003, and references therein, p. 488).

2. Negative autocorrelation of individual stock returns over short horizons (Jegadeesh and Titman, 1995; Conrad et al., 1991; Jegadeesh,1990; Kaul and Nimalendran, 1990; Lehmann, 1990). Large firms exhibit weaker negative

autocorrelation than the smaller firms. Kaul and Nimalendran (1990) show that some large firms on NYSE exhibit positive autocorrelation.

3. Positive autocorrelation of portfolio returns over short (weekly or monthly) horizons (Boulatov et al., 2013; Conrad et al., 1991; Lo and MacKinlay, 1988). The extent of positive autocorrelation is inversely related to firm size.

4. Positive autocorrelation of stock returns over medium (3- to 12-month) horizons (Jegadeesh and Titman, 2001; Rouwenhorst, 1999, 1998; Jegadeesh and Titman, 1993).

5. Negative autocorrelation of stock returns over long (2- to 5-year) horizons (Chopra et al., 1992; De Bondt and Thaler, 1987, 1985).

6. Stock returns of large firms predict returns of smaller firms, but not vice versa (Lo and MacKinlay, 1988).

7. Positive relation between institutional ownership and contemporaneous stock returns (Sias et al. 2006).

2.2 Inventory costs based microstructure models

Garman (1976) is the first who modeled the market in a stochastic way and modeled the supply and demand of the stock. His method is followed by many subsequent papers, including Amihud and Mendelson (1980) and Ho and Stoll (1981). Notice that Garman's (1976) method is very useful to depict the inventory development and the order sequence (Amihud and Mendelson, 1980, p. 5).

Ho and Stoll (1981) are of the flavor of portfolio theory. The dealer has base wealth, which is invested in the most efficient portfolio for the dealer. At the beginning of making a market, the dealer has no inventory nor cash. We can imagine the dealer obtains the cash needed to make the market by loans with their base wealth as collateral. In a multi-period context, the dealer optimizes the total portfolio. The trade-off facing the dealer is that inventory always pushes the dealer away from the efficient portfolio. So spread is charged on transactions as compensation to the dealer's service. As the time evolves, the dealer becomes more and more concerned about the terminal wealth. However, at the beginning of the time, the dealer is less concerned about it, rather he is concerned about the fees he charges. The conclusion is that the spread is independent of the dealer's inventory position; and the dealer encourages his customers to trade in his desired direction by changing the midpoint of the spread, rather than by changing the spread size itself.

Ho and Stoll (1981) incorporate many institutional characteristics, especially modeling the market as the combination of call and continuous auction markets. In their model, the limit orders arrive completely exogenously, while some of the market orders arrive exogenously, and the rest of the market orders are price dependent. Moreover, the limit orders arrive according to the linear regression function, and the same is true for the market orders. These regression functions can also be viewed in this way. The forthcoming market orders are unknown to the market maker when he sets the bid and ask prices. The expected future market order flows are defined by this function. For the limit orders, they are exogenous, therefore they are actually arriving according to the regression function. In this sense, this function implies a more rigorous restriction. Furthermore, neither the market maker's anticipation nor the pattern of limit orders' arrival vary over time or circumstances. In this sense, there is no interactions between informed and uninformed traders. Notice it is true that a linear regression result can be derived from any data. However, the linear function characterizing the limit and market order's arrivals is true only in statistical regression sense. It remains unclear whether the optimal pricing policy under this function is also optimal under the true order arrival function. Therefore, it casts some doubts on the generality the authors claim for their model.

However, the model does shed new insights. It emphasizes that the market maker faces another uncertainty, namely the future order flows. In setting a higher (ask) price, the market maker is trading off between higher cash flow profit and larger inventory (see the objective function, i.e. equation 6 on page 9). Notice the inventory has two sources of positive utility for the market maker. One is the interest earned from lending stocks, and the other is the larger stocks inventory with more assets. The latter is not free from controversy. Generally speaking, this model belongs to the school of inventory costs, and it does not attempt to account for the information-based trading.

2.3 Information based microstructure models

If we allow some market participants do have private information, then what interests us is how this private information is incorporated into the prices. Bagehot (1971) is the seminal work that explicitly discusses the information-based trading. Later on Kyle (1985) is undoubtedly the most important work in this area. The following papers deal with the topic of private information and bid-ask spread: Glosten and Milgrom (1985) and Easley and O'Hara (1987). Of course Kyle (1985) is very famous on this topic. Of note is that only one informed trader is allowed in Kyle's (1985) model, where the informed trader enjoys some sort of monopoly power on his private information. Holden and Subrahmanyam (1992) generalize Kyle's (1985) model to allow multiple informed traders. Admati and Pfleiderer (1988) provides another extension.

Glosten and Milgrom (1985) study the bid-ask spread from the perspective of quotation revision dynamics. The key assumption/conclusion is that the market maker updates the quote after every trade occurs. A buy order leads an upward updating of the ask price, and a sell order leads a downward updating for the bid price. In other words, the market maker is updating their quotation as if the next order comes from an informed investor, although in a probabilistic view. Thus, the amount of updating depends on the market maker's expected probability of the next order being informed. This quotation updating feature can also be well explained by Ho and Stoll (1981) and O'Hara and Oldfield (1986). One of the motives of the authors' writing this paper may be to tell an adverse selection version of the story, differentiated from the inventory version provided by prior models. They tell an inventory-rebalancing story. This paper offers an insight; the bid (ask) price is set according to the expectation conditioning on all the public information and the "fact" that someone, maybe informed, values the stock lower (higher) and thus is willing to sell (buy) on this price. Several predictions and insights of this model are noteworthy. First, if we assume that the informed trader's trading activity is positively related with trading volume, then lagged volume will be positively related with the spread. Second, the reason why adverse selection problem does not lead the stock market to break down is due to the inelasticity of the liquidity investor's demand and supply. Third, average volume is proportional to one over squared average spread. The order-handling cost story predicts a similar relation, although volume is proportional to one over spread, rather than squared spread. This feature predicts that larger volume is related to smaller spread. Fourth, the relation indicated in the previous feature implies that with more trading volume, the spread approaches to zero. The interpretation of this feature is that given that no new information comes to the market, the expectation of both the market maker and the liquidity investors converges to that of the informed trader's.

Overall, Glosten and Milgrom (1985) formalize the quotation revision dynamics, which explains how the private information is assimilated by the market. The market maker updates the bid and ask prices after every transaction occurs as if the order is placed by an informed trader (in this sense, the model of Glosten and Milgrom (1985) has some Bayesian flavor). The price will be updated to the point that equates the informed trader's expectation conditioning on his private information. Although succinct, this model does have some places that can be extended. In this model, the market maker is taking a naive and passive way to update the quotation. He makes no efforts to identify the informed trader. Furthermore, only market orders are allowed. Thus, the key extension will come from the discussion of optimal trading strategy of informed traders.

Easley and O'Hara (1987) contend that trade size plays roles when market makers set prices. The general idea is that, for multiple informed traders, trading large size always (weakly) dominates other actions. Thus trading size is naturally related to informed trading. Taking this into account, market makers update their belief and therefore set prices by observing the trade size. They work out two equilibriums, namely pooling equilibrium and separating equilibrium. In separating equilibrium, the informed traders always trade large sizes. To formalize the conditions for the existence of pooling and separating equilibrium, the authors propose two concepts: market width and depth. The former refers to the ratio of large to small trade size. The latter refers to the fraction of large trades made by uninformed traders. When the market has sufficiently large width or few informed traders, the separating equilibrium will prevail; the pooling equilibrium will prevail otherwise. Several points are noteworthy. First, the authors make it clear that both the trade size and trade sequence play roles in determining prices and price impacts. The trade sequence is important because market makers dynamically update their beliefs. Second, the authors point out that market makers face another uncertainty, namely the occurrence of the event. Third, the authors argue that midpoints might be biased as the proxy for the market price, since the spread needs not be symmetric around the true market price. If the price is set based on the order size, it is possible that there is more block trades on one side. However, the direction of this bias is unclear. Overall, the view held by the authors is that stock prices respond to all the factors including transaction costs, inventory costs, and the adverse selection costs. However, this chapter focuses on the adverse selection only.

Private information and inventory consideration can both affect prices. Hasbrouck (1988), Hasbrouck (1999) provides a model to incorporate both considerations. Glosten and Harris (1988) and Hasbrouck (1988, 1991a, b) provide some empirical evidences (see also Madhavan and Smidt, 1993).

Another interesting—yet sparsely investigated—issue is whether market makers have private information. Most models assume that market makers do not possess private information. Empirical investigations can be conducted on whether market makers are uninformed as we had thought. See Anand et al. (2011, p. 199) for some arguments that market makers could be informed. Manaster et al. (1999) also show that market making is not the main source of market makers' profits.

2.4 What is risk?

Wagner (2011) proposes a notion of "joint liquidation risk." If you are forced to liquidate a position at fire sale prices, it is probably because other investors are also forced to do so. Therefore, it is optimal, at least for the liquidation prone investors, to hold portfolios that are distinguished from others. In this sense, market portfolio incurs a joint liquidation risk when all the investors hold market portfolio. The author further argues that idiosyncratic risk should be priced as it provides investors with "diversity" (compared with the diversified portfolios widely held by all investors).

Favara et al. (2012) explore the idea that shareholders can strategically default and by doing so they can affect the equity risk (see the cited papers for more studies on strategic default). Conventional finance theory suggests that idiosyncratic risk should not be priced. However, there are reasons to believe that idiosyncratic risk plays a role in asset pricing. Bartram et al. (2012, p. 1330) mention these reasons. For idiosyncratic risk to be priced, limit of arbitrage provides crucial conditions. Gromb and Vayanos (2010) review the literature on limit of arbitrage.

Ben-David et al. (2012, p. 1) contend that "hedge funds are the investor class that most closely resembles textbook arbitrageurs." But hedge funds heavily rely on outside funding, which creates a limit for them to arbitrage. Ben-David et al. (2012) demonstrate that during the recent financial crisis, investors withdrew money from the hedge funds, causing the funds able to arbitrage and thus exit the U.S. market. This idea is treated in the models provided by Shleifer and Vishny (1997), Gromb and Vayanos (2002), and Brunnermeier and Pedersen (2009). Notably, these three models, especially the latter two, emphasize the limit of arbitrage caused by the lack of capital on the part of arbitrageurs.

2.5 Trading mechanism

This question is important partly because the U.S. stock market thrives as a leading representative of a quote driven market despite the popularity of the limit order markets due to the advance of electronic technology. Besides, the limit order market has a "good" feature that the order book is often open to all the investors, thus the liquidity provision is competitive. In contrast, a quote driven market is often characterized as an opaque limit order book, accessible only to the market maker which provides liquidity in a monopoly manner. One strand of study argues that order driven market has features dominating the quote driven market. The other strand defends the quote driven market by arguing that the quote driven market has some characteristics that the order driven market does not have.

Glosten (1994) directly asks "Is the electronic open limit order book inevitable?" His answer is yes because he argues that open limit order market is more robust to competition from other markets. Back and Baruch (2007) compare a limit order market with a floor exchange. A floor exchange is neither a limit order market nor a pure dealer market. Here by "dealer market" I mean a market in which a market maker posts quotes and stands ready to trade against any market orders. On a floor exchange, the incoming order is revealed, and the dealers compete with each other to fill the order. Typically the incoming order is exposed to all the floor traders to ensure the competition.

In late 1990s, the Chicago Mercantile Exchange (CME) introduced the electronic GLOBEX trading system as a complement to its open outcry trading. The instrument traded on GLOBEX is identical to the future contracts in the open outcry market, except that GLOBEX trade smaller size contracts, i.e., E-mini. Kurov and Lasser (2004) show that for the contracts traded on both systems, Emini has dominant contributions to the price discovery, and the trades initiated by exchange locals in the E-mini contracts are more informative than the off-exchange initiated trades. Their evidences are consistent with Hasbrouck (2003).

Masulis and Shivakumar (2002) compare the price adjustment speed on NYSE/AMEX and Nasdaq. The former has a lower speed. Further, the authors provide detailed comparisons about different trading mechanisms on these markets (see pp. 619–620).

2.6 Short selling

Lamont (2012, pp. 3–5) discusses the mechanism of short selling and its constraint. He provides a good discussion on the short sellers' trade off of whether to maintain secrecy (see p. 4).

Short selling is difficult even in the U.S.. For example: "Almazan et al. (2004) find that only about 30% of mutual funds are allowed to sell short, and only 2% actually do sell short." In crisis, for example, wars and the likes of the 9/11 attack, short selling is banned (Lamont, 2012).

A key principle of Harrison and Kreps's (1978) model is that the optimist always sets the price if short selling is prohibited. Lamont (2012, pp. 5–6) gives a simple example illustrating Harrison and Kreps's (1978) model.

One theme of short selling studies is that short selling constraints lead to overpricing. Prior literature (see the papers cited by Lamont (2012, p. 7) on short selling constraints by the costs of shorting, or indirectly by breadth of ownership and short interests and Lamont and Thaler (2003) discussing the problems with using short interests as a proxy). In other words, there is a negative relation between short selling activities and subsequent stock returns.

Short sellers are informed (Senchack and Starks, 1993; Asquith et al., 2005; Boehmer et al., 2008; Engelberg, Reed, and Ringgenberg; 2012), given predictability of short selling on subsequent stock returns. An alternative explanation is that short sellers spread false rumors to manipulate prices.

The overpricing story assumes that short sellers are right. Lamont (2012, p. 8) quotes a short seller saying that "we can look at a company that is attacking us. When we have the goods on that company, it tells us we are onto something. The louder they scream, the better the short." The companies whose managers believe they are undervalued are not likely to take anti short selling actions.

2.7 Other topics in microstructure

Hasbrouck and Saar (2009) show that one third of limit orders are canceled within two seconds. They attribute these "fleeting orders" to market order investors' searching for latent liquidity. The existence of fleeting limit orders challenges the traditional assumption that only liquidity investors use limit orders.

Foucault et al. (2005, p. 1172), building on previous literature, propose three dimensions of market quality:

a liquid market [is] (a) tight-small spreads, (b) deep-small price impact, and (c) resilient-prices recover quickly after liquidity demand shocks.

Biais et al. (1995) study the resiliency of the market. As for resilience, Foucault et al. (2005) provide a theoretical model.

Bid ask spread is transaction cost borne by investors. Thus, it's an important dimension of execution quality of the exchange. Other dimensions of execution quality exist as well. Boehmer (2005) argues that, besides transaction costs, investors also care about transaction speed. His argument explains why some investors choose NASDAQ, which has higher transaction costs than NYSE does. That is because NASDAQ executes faster.

Cao et al. (2000) study the pre-open quotations on Nasdaq. They use the crossed/locked inside quotes to proxy the information contents of pre-open quotations. They provide a detailed discussion on the institutions of Nasdaq preopen quotations. They also discuss why NASDAQ market makers communicate via the quotation system to reveal their information and identity to reach an open price that incorporates all the available information (see pp. 1344–1346). That is because such an informative open price benefits all the market makers, and the revealed identity assures that each market maker reveals its true information.

Madhavan and Panchapagesan (2000) provide institution details of NYSE opening, which is a typical auction market where the specialist sets the open price. A key feature of NYSE opening is that the specialist sets the price and participates in trading at the same time. It may raise the question whether the specialist sets the open price honestly. Madhavan and Panchapagesan (2002, 2000) give affirmative answers to this question.

Hendershott et al. (2011) use the number of message traffics to proxy algorithmic trading. The authors show that algorithmic trading enhances liquidity. See Section I of this paper for the literature on this issue. The authors also discuss several scenarios in which algorithmic trading is used. By using algorithmic trading, some hedge funds and broker-dealers supply liquidity, some traders can find better liquidity, some traders can arbitrage among different trading venues, institutional investors trade large quantities of stocks gradually, or some traders simply find the patterns of the orders and trade on this.

Chapter 3 Liquidity

3.1 Measuring liquidity

Liquidity is an important feature of any financial market. Therefore there have been a lot of literature trying to understand liquidity. To understand liquidity, first we need to measure liquidity.

As Jeremy (2007, p. 3) observes, Kyle's (1985) concept of liquidity consists of three aspects: tightness, depth, and resiliency. Besides these three measures of liquidity, Amihud (2002) proposes an illiquidity measurement. Duarte and Young's (2009) PSOS can also be a proxy of illiquidity. Other measurements are: size, turnover, opening spread. Because intraday data are available only recently, to cover a longer period, we have to use some liquidity proxies which can be computed using daily data. Amihud's (2002) illiquidity measurement is one of them. Goyenko et al. (2009) investigate how well these daily proxies are doing their jobs.

The above measurements of liquidity can be called "direct" measures in the sense that they are derived from the original meaning of liquidity. However, they are not the most widely used liquidity measurements. The most widely used measurements are bid-ask spreads and PIN. But one should keep in mind that bid-ask spreads and PIN are also associated with asymmetric information.

Market makers and liquidity investors indicate their intention to provide liquidity via quotes. So quotes are important in understanding price dynamics. Quotes have three dimensions: midpoint (location), spread (width), and depth (shares at each price). These dimensions reflect different views of liquidity providers. Midpoint reflects liquidity providers' expectation of the stock's fundamental value. Spread and depth reflect the uncertainty about the fundamental value (Chung et al., 2008).

Bid-ask spread is the compensation for market maker's providing liquidity. Along this line, some empirical literatures have shown that the bid-ask spread is determined by such factors as volume, risk, price, and firm size. Bid-ask spreads measure the transaction costs, which is a major market friction. Bid-ask spread and the short-term return predictability are explored by Roll (1984), Stoll (1989), Huang and Stoll (1997), and Madhavan et al. (1997).

Jang and Venkatesh (1991) test the assumption of bid-ask spread models that when there is a transaction, both bid and ask price will change by the same amount, thus leaving the width of the spread unchanged. They show that quote revision depends on the level of spread and the transaction size. When the spread is larger than three-eighths, 70% of the transactions are followed by change in both bid and ask price, and the spread is more likely to be decreased on the next quoter evision than increased. Whereas when the spread is lower than two-eighths, there are less than 10% of the transactions followed by both changes, and the spread is more likely to be increased. And when the outstanding spread is one-eighth, then the normal quote-midpoint change would be zero.

The microstructure model of PIN was first proposed by Easley et al. (1997). But the term "PIN" did not appear until Easley et al. (2002). Bernhardt and Hughson (2002) provide a similar model which accounts for the order size. Easley et al. (2008) extend the original PIN model by a GARCH specification to allow for a time-varying arrival rate of informed and uninformed traders. Easley et al. (2012) further refine the PIN idea.

Easley and O'Hara (2004) argue that PIN can explain expected return, because it's a proxy of asymmetric information. Easley et al. (2002) and O'Hara (2003) also discuss the relation between asymmetric information and asset pricing. Duarte and Young (2009) counter-argue that PIN is priced not because it is a proxy of asymmetric information, but because it is a proxy of illiquidity. Mohanram and Rajgopal (2009) show that PIN is not priced if one extends Easley et al.'s (2002) sample period.

Besides bid-ask spreads and PIN, price impact can also be linked to liquidity, hence is a measurement of liquidity. However, price impact can be further dissected into two parts: transitory versus permanent price impacts. Permanent price impact is associated with asymmetric information, and is systemically associated with order size and firm capitalization. This topic is discussed in block-trade (Barclay and Holderness, 1992; Keim and Madhavan, 1996).

3.2 Volume

The first question about volume is that where does it come from. This indeed is a question because traditional asset pricing models leave little room for the existence of volume. These models often assume a representative agent. With only one investor on the market, we can say nothing about trading volume. Some models allow heterogeneity in the investors, for example, heterogeneous utility functions, initial endowments, labor income, etc. As Judd et al. (2003) show, such heterogeneity does not necessarily cause trading in general equilibrium in a complete market. They suggest that "life-cycle factors, asymmetric information, heterogeneous belief, and incompleteness of the asset market" are more likely to be the causes of trading (p. 2216).

In theoretical perspectives, volume is an important source of public information for uninformed investors, in that it conveys information about the private signal received by informed investors. Most models decode the information conveyed by the volume by updating the belief to the same direction of the trading volume. Llorente et al. (2002) provide a different insight by arguing that the traders may have different motivations to trade. If the trade is motivated by non-informational reasons, referred to as hedging trades by the authors, then the price dynamics are return reversion. On the contrary, if the trade is motivated by informational reasons, referred to as speculative trades, the price exhibits positive autocorrelation. Another insight is that when information becomes public suddenly and no one knows the information before publication, the information changes the stock price, but doesn't change the demand of the stock, therefore there's no abnormal volume related to the information.

Kandel and Pearson (1995, pp. 844–847) discuss various reasons of trading. They offer a model in which different interpretation of public information leads to abnormal trading. They show that if investors have identical likelihood function, i.e., they interpret signals identically, then the revision of belief should neither flip (cross, i.e., prior relative pessimists become optimists, and vice versa) nor diverge (the difference between pessimists and optimists becomes larger), and the mean revision should be in the same direction, see Proposition 1 and 2 on p. 852 of their text. Bamber et al. (1999) provide evidence supporting Kandel and Pearson's (1995) conclusion.

Hong and Stein (2003) combine heterogeneous belief and limits of arbitrage, and propose a model relating to volatility and volume. This idea dates back to Miller (1977). Chen et al. (2001) provide supportive evidence. Grundy and McNichols's (1989) model also show that there is trading even without new information. Grundy and Kim (2002) numerically test the idea.

In Suominen's (2001) model, "availability of private information" determines the probability of informed trading. Liquidity traders respond to the probability of informed trading by changing their own order placement strategy, i.e., liquidity traders place more market orders when informed trading is fewer, and vice versa. Availability of private information changes over time, but with positive autocorrelation (see p. 548). This autocorrelation helps liquidity traders predict the probability of informed trading. In this sense, volume is related with PIN. Notice that his model has implications on daily PIN variation, which is seldom a focus in empirical research.

Volume is close related to liquidity, although the relation between them is not monotonic. Lo and Wang (2000) discuss the various measures of volume in their Table 1. They argue that turnover should be the preferred measure of trading activity.

In NYSE/Amex, transactions are recorded once. In NASDAQ, transactions are recorded twice. So to compare turnover or volume across NYSE and NASDAQ, we need to double the volume for all NYSE and Amex stocks. Examples of this adjustment are LaPlante and Muscarella (1997) and Loughran and Schultz (2005).

Volume is positively related to contemporaneous and future stock return volatility (Karpoff, 1987; Lamoureux and Lastrapes, 1990). Kandel and Pearson (1995, Figure. 1 on p. 839) find that the abnormal volume is only marginally related with the magnitude of the returns and the most striking evidence is that there is abnormal volume even the return is zero. These evidences are inconsistent with the prior model's prediction that higher stock returns are accompanied with high abnormal volume.

3.3 Determinants of liquidity

Chordia et al. (2005) discuss the determinants of spread. Their regression becomes standard in discussing spread. Hameed et al. (2010) use their results to detrend (clean) the raw spreads (eq. 1 on pp. 262). The eq. 2 on p. 265 of their text also lists the potential factors determining the stock's spread.

The determinants of liquidity can be categorized into the following groups:

1. Firm specific variations: price, volume, volatility.

2. Firm's sensitivities to market wide liquidity (sometimes is also referred to as liquidity beta): Chordia et al. (2000, 2005); Coughenour and Saad (2004).

3. Exchange level variations. Brockman et al. (2009).

4. Location. Loughran and Schultz (2005) show that compared with urban stocks, rural stocks are traded less, and have less analyst coverage.

5. Awareness of investors. Seasholes and Zhu (2010); Grullon et al. (2004); Frieder and Subrahmanyam (2005).

6. Heflin and Shaw (2000) show that the existence of the blockholder harms liquidity.

7. Chung et al. (2010) show the good corporate governance enhances liquidity.

For the determinants of depth, see Brockman and Chung (1999). Technology also plays some role in determining liquidity. Hendershott et al. (2011) investigate whether algorithmic trading increases or decreases liquidity.

Another way to find the determinants of liquidity is to dig the commonality of liquidity across stocks, and maybe across countries. For this see Chordia et al. (2000), Hasbrouck and Seppi (2001), Huberman and Halka (2001), Brockman and Chung (2002), Fabre and Frino (2004), Coughenour and Saad (2004), Domowitz et al. (2005), Mitchell et al. (2007), Korajczyk and Sadka (2008), and Brockman et al. (2009).

Corwin and Lipson (2011) show that program traders and the institutional traders are the main reasons driving the commonality of stock return and liquidity. They also discuss alternative explanations (behavioral explanations) on pp. 50–52 of their text.

3.4 Markets' and liquidity providers' conditions and liquidity

Asymmetry information is not the only story behind liquidity. Even the liquidity providers are comfortable with the level of asymmetric information; variations of their capital position and revenues will change their willingness to provide liquidity. Theories on the non-asymmetry information stories have been developed by Kyle and Xiong (2001), Gromb and Vayanos (2002), and Brunnermeier and Pedersen (2009), among others.

In extreme events of market decline, there is a famous fact called "flight to liquidity" (Brunnermeier and Pedersen, 2009). Hameed et al. (2010) empirically show that market decline will tighten the liquidity. They attribute this effect to the dry-up of liquidity providers' funding. That is, these investors are capital constrained during the market decline. They discuss three proxies of capital constraint on p. 272 of their text.

Reinforcing Hameed et al.'s (2010) arguments, Khandani and Lo (2011) show that the forced liquidation of some sizable hedge fund beginning on August 6, 2007 sets a spiral which finally dries up the "market making risk capital" of hedge funds. An implicit assumption of Khandani and Lo (2011) is that these hedge funds are major players of providing liquidity, whereas in Hameed et al. (2010) it's the dealers that are providing liquidity. Another insight of Khandani and Lo (2011) is that the so-called market neutral long/short equity funds are actually inherently instable, they are vulnerable to small shocks, even shocks beyond equity markets. The pervasive existence of long/short hedge funds contributes to systematic risk, in that they are important to maintain market liquidity.

Comerton-Forde et al. (2010) also empirically explore the capital limits of the specialists and liquidity. Concretely, the wealth (revenue) and the capital committed (inventories) play significant roles in determining liquidity. The following authors discuss the revenues of specialists: Hasbrouck and Sofianos (1993) and Panayides (2007).

Note that the above line of discussion on liquidity differs subtly from the bidask spread liquidity discussion. Acharya and Viswanathan (2011, p. 100) define two types of liquidity, both of which are closely related to the recent financial crisis, that is, the market liquidity and funding liquidity. The market liquidity is "the ease of selling assets at fair prices" whereas the funding liquidity is "the ease of rolling over existing debt."

3.5 The effect of liquidity on the firm's well-being

The liquidity affects the cost of capital (Amihud, 2002). Eckbo and Norli (2005) find that firms issuing equity are more liquid, and if controlled for this liquidity factor, the underperformance of issuing firms disappears. Butler et al. (2005) and Butler and Wan (2010) show empirical evidence that liquid stocks have lower cost of issuing new equity and bond, respectively.

Why does a liquid stock have lower return? See Amihud and Mendelson (1986a, b). Also see Merton (1987) for explanation that people only invest on securities which they are familiar with, so a larger investor base gives rise to a lower capital cost. Denis and Mihov (2003) and Odders-White and Ready (2006) show that liquid stocks have better credit quality, and are more likely to issue debts.

Kedia and Panchapagesan (2011) show that firms move from NASDAQ to NYSE to exploit the lower cost capital and to facilitate the corporate transactions in the coming years. Their evidence, on the one hand, are consistent with the Amihud's (2002) argument; on the hand, their evidence imply that moving to NYSE is driven by the potential transactions, and not all eligible firms move.

Fang et al. (2009) shows the causality that higher liquidity increases stock's market value. Lipson and Mortal (2009) show that the firms with more liquid stocks have lower debt-to-asset ratio, and prefer equity financing. Their evidence is consistent with the notion that liquidity reduces capital costs.

Besides the governmental rules, some firms impose their regulations on insider trading, most of them being a blackout period. Bettis et al. (2000) found that the stocks of these firms have fewer insider trading, and narrower spread.

3.6 Who is providing liquidity

The willingness of investors, be they dealers or institutional investors or individual investors, to provide liquidity is by every means the most fundamental factor determining liquidity. To understand what affects this willingness, we need to know who they are in the first place. In a dealer's market, dealers are arguably the most important, or to be more accurate, the most investigated, group of investors of providing liquidity. So it's trivial to ask who is providing liquidity on dealer's market. But this question is not trivial with respect to the order-driven market.

Adverse selection cost borne of providing liquidity is a plausible concern of the liquidity providers. Yet, I highly doubt it's the sole explanation. While facing asymmetric information, liquidity providers are making profit, at least in microstructure theories. Then what factors may affect this profit making process?

Aggarwal and Angel (1999) argue that dealers do not necessarily "hate" wider bid-ask spread. On the contrary, a smaller spread is less likely to motivate dealers to provide liquidity. It is the lack of such incentive that doomed the ECM, which is designed to offer a trading platform for small and illiquid stocks. Lay people may hate risks, but those who make a living on risks love risks.

Besides the traditional belief that dealers are providing liquidity, Khandani and Lo (2011) show that hedge funds are also providing liquidity.

Since the non-dealer liquidity providers can both take and supply liquidity, it's important to understand their limit versus market order decision. When do they provide, and when do they take liquidity? Corwin and Lipson (2011) and Domowitz et al. (2005) provide some discussion on this topic.

Behavioral explanations are also helpful in understanding the fundamental utility function of individual investors. For example, Guiso et al. (2008) show that mistrust hampers people participating in investing in the stock market. Other cognitive biases, such as local bias, may also help explain the participation in the stock investment.

Besides the market makers, limit order submitters also provide liquidity. There is evidence of hedge funds providing liquidity. Aitken et al. (2007) use a unique data set showing that institutional investors, i.e., proprietary trading desks, hedge funds, mutual funds, index funds, and insurance companies, do provide liquidity. They place limit orders at multiple prices. Furthermore, unlike designated market makers who are trading on both sides, Aitken et al. (2007, p. 145) show that it is the standard practice for these institutional investors to supply liquidity on one side of the book only.

In recent years, the rise of high-frequency trading has dramatically changed the landscape of liquidity provision. Notice that "high-frequency trading firms represent approximately 2% of the nearly 20,000 trading firms operating in the U. S. markets, but since 2009 they have accounted for over 70% of the volume in U.S. equity markets and are fast approaching 50% of the volume in futures markets" (Easley et al., 2012, p. 1457).

Chapter 4
Limit orders

4.1 The models of limit orders

Unlike early microstructure model heavily relying on asymmetric information, it seems that recent literature on the order driven market deliberately ignores this feature, and chooses "patience/impatience" as the backbone of their modeling. For example, Foucault et al. (2005, p. 1174) argue that it often makes the model intractable if accounting for the asymmetric information. They further argue that Huang and Stoll's (1997) empirical work shows that asymmetric information accounts for a smaller, less than 20%, of the total bid-ask spread. Similarly, Roşu (2009, p. 4602) argues that "asymmetric information is hard to measure and is usually unobservable." So we will discuss the patience story in this subsection, and postpone the discussion on the asymmetric information story for the next subsection.

In terms of the investor's utility, a limit order promises a better price, but delayed or even unsuccessful execution, whereas a market order guarantees the immediate execution, but at a poorer price. So choice between limit and market orders boils down to the trade-off between waiting costs and better price. Naturally, the patience of an investor is the most influential factor of the waiting costs. It is unsurprising that most of the models use patience to explain the limit versus market order choice. We will discuss this question in more detail later on.

Notably, the patience also determines the price at which to place the limit order. For example, Roşu's (2009) model proposes a utility function for a limit sell order submitter:

$$f_t = \mathbb{E}_t\big(P_\tau - \tilde{r}(\tau - t)\big) \tag{4.1}$$

where f_t denotes the seller's utility at time t, P_τ denotes the price of limit sell order, $\tilde{r}$ denotes the seller's patience coefficient[1] and τ denotes the time at which the order is executed. In Eq. 4.1, we can assume that only τ is a random variable. Therefore, the utility function can be further written as:

$$f_t = P_\tau - \tilde{r}(\mathbb{E}_t(\tau) - t) \tag{4.2}$$

Eq. 4.2 shows that the longer the expected waiting time, the lower the utility. So with the number of limit order submitters increasing, all the limit order submitters are strictly worse off.

Roşu (2009) models the price dynamics in a world without asymmetric information. He argues that investors have the same expected utility on the same side, despite placing orders at different prices. They have same expected utility because their utility function consists of two parts: the level of execution price and the waiting cost. Take an example of the ask side. Higher ask prices increase the first component of the utility function, while decreasing the second component of the utility function. Thus, in equilibrium, all the investors on the same side of the limit order book have the same expected utility. In summary, Roşu's (2009) main conclusions are as follows:

1. As the number of limit order submitters increases, the spread narrows down (p. 4610).
2. When the patient investors arrive faster than impatient investors, the limit order book is resilient (p. 4614).
3. The mean spread decreases with competition of patient and impatient investors, defined as $c = \frac{\lambda_P}{\lambda_{IP}}$, where λ_P, λ_{IP} denotes the arrival rates of patient and impatient investors, respectively. In other words, when the patient investors arrive faster, the spread is smaller, whereas when the impatient investors arrive faster, the spread is larger. Also notice that Roşu's (2009) definition of "competition" refers to the competition among patient investors, and it is in relative sense, i.e., it is relative to the arrival rate of impatient

1 It may be more appropriate to call $r^\sim$ *impatient coefficient*, because the larger $r^\sim$ is, the more impatient the investor.

investors. So when the impatient investors arrive faster, the competition among patient investors decreases. It makes sense that when there are more market orders, the patient investors compete less for the market orders. See Proposition 2 on p. 4614 of Rosu's text.

4. The mean spread increases granularity $\epsilon = \frac{r}{\lambda_P + \lambda_{IP}}$, , where r denotes the patience coefficient, and recall that the larger r means the investors are more impatient. It means that the mean spread narrows down when the investors are more patient, and when the activity of either patient or impatient investors increases. But, it is unclear how spread changes when there are more impatient investors, because it has two opposite effects on the spread. First, the increase in impatient investors increases the activity, and therefore decreases the spread. Second, the increases in impatient investors *de facto* reduces the competition among patient investors, and thus increases spread. Roşu (2009, last paragraph on p. 4615) argues that the effect via total activity does not dominate unless the impatient investors are very rare; see proposition 2 on p. 4614, and discussions on p. 4615).

5. The activity decreases the volatility of the asset. See Proposition 3 on p. 4616 of Rosu's text (2009).

6. Roşu (2009) discusses multi-unit market orders in Section 4 from p. 4618. His multi-unit market order amounts to a liquidity shock in Foucault et al.'s (2005) sense. When a multi-unit market order arrives, while the limit orders are still restricted to one unit, it first consumes several limit orders, resulting in an instantaneous price impact. Because the limit order submitters are allowed to cancel and resubmit their unfilled orders, they strategically reshape the limit order books after this liquidity shock, resulting in a subsequent, or permanent price impact. Notably, this instantaneous price impact is mechanical, and this permanent price impact has nothing to do with asymmetric information. Roşu (2009, p. 4621) shows that instantaneous price impact is larger than the permanent price impact, meaning a price overshooting.[2] The instantaneous price impact is a convex function of the order size. However, when we consider the shape of the limit order book, the instantaneous price impact can be any shape. Roşu (2009, p. 4624) shows that when the large market order is very likely, the limit orders cluster at some point above the ask price, so the instantaneous price impact is concave; and when the large market order is not likely, the limit orders cluster at the ask

2 The notion of resiliency also implies the price overshooting.

price, so the instantaneous price impact is convex.

7. Roşu (2009) predicts a "comovement" of bid and ask prices. That is, bid and ask prices move in the same direction when a market order changes the price on either side. For example, when a market sell order consumes all the limit orders at the bid price, the bid price mechanically moves downward. Then the limit buy order submitters reshape the ask side of the book, and the new ask price also moves downward. But the movement of ask price is smaller than the bid price, therefore the spread widens immediately after this execution. This comovement has nothing to do with asymmetric information. Another model generating similar results is Parlour (1998, proposition 6, p. 806). The empirical evidence of comovement was first found by Biais et al. (1995), but they attributed it to the asymmetric information.

Foucault et al. (2005) model a non-asymmetric information world. Under certain assumptions (p. 1176), they show that the spread interacts with the expected waiting cost. If the expected waiting cost is smaller, for example, there are more impatient investors, the patient investors are less likely to post aggressive prices. Spread improvement is a measure of the liquidity provider's aggressiveness. They also explore an important dimension of market quality resilience.

Glosten (1994) proposes one of the earliest structural models on the price dynamics in a limit order market. He argues that the prices on the limit order book are posted in a "regret free" manner. In his model, order size is endogenous. That is, the investor chooses the optimal order size to maximize her utility. de Jong et al. (1996) extend Glosten's (1994) model. The following models also account for the asymmetric information: de Jong et al. (1996), Goettler et al. (2009), and Roşu (2010).

4.2 Investor's choice of limit versus market orders

If we assume no asymmetric information, the choice between limit versus market orders is usually reduced to a simple dichotomy. That is, patient investors place limit orders, while impatient investors place market orders. Foucault et al. (2005, p. 1176) justify this idea by arguing that value traders (such as portfolio managers), who trade due to the long-term fundamental value, can be viewed as patient investors; whereas the arbitrageurs, index traders, and technical traders can be viewed as impatient investors. They also argue that Keim and Madhavan's (1995) empirical evidence supports this idea.

Kaniel and Liu (2006) develop a model showing that "if the probability of the [private] information long lived is high, then informed traders more likely place limit orders than market orders; and the expected time horizon of the informed traders' private information is critical for the choice of limit orders versus market orders" (p. 1868). They also show that the information horizon is negatively related to the bid ask spread, because longer horizon implies the informed traders are less likely to place market orders, thus the market maker is facing a smaller adverse selection cost. They also notice that the reverse of the above causality holds as well, i.e., when the spread is narrower, the benefit of price improvement of a limit order is smaller, thus it makes the limit orders less attractive. The empirical evidence in their paper shows that general informed investors prefer placing limit orders, and the limit orders convey more information than do market orders.

Notably, Economides and Schwartz's (1995) survey data show that "two thirds of the respondents indicate that they are willing to trade patiently to reduce execution costs" and "nearly two-thirds regularly or frequently use limit orders." Economides and Schwartz (1995, p. 5) argue that "investment decisions commonly involve information gathering and analysis, and the entire process can take over a period of several days." They further ask: "Is it likely the value of a decision made over a period of a day or more can decay within the span of an hour or less?" Bloomfield et al. (2005) use an experiment to show the informed investor uses market order early in the trading session, and uses limit orders later. They show also that informed investors prefer limit orders in general. Goettler et al. (2009) show that both informed and uninformed investors place limit orders.

Most of the researchers believe most individual investors use limit orders. Linnainmaa (2010) investigates individual investors' trading behavior in Finland and show that "76.3% of individuals' orders are limit orders" and "individuals may not always actively monitor their limit orders, [because] first, individuals submit 22% of their limit orders before the trading session starts, and second, individuals often leave their orders in the limit order book for several days" (p. 1478).

4.3 Limit order revisions and aggressiveness

Noticeably, the above models either allow no order revision after the limit order is submitted, or assume no cost for revising the limit order. But in reality, to revise the limit order in a timely manner after every change in the market situation, it entails the investors to monitor the market continuously, which inevitably incurs a large cost. Therefore limit order submitters face another risk[3]: "picked-off risk" (also known as "free trading option risk") if they do not closely monitor the market. Otherwise, to completely avoid this risk, the investors have to accept the cost of continuously monitoring the market.

Ellul et al. (2007) look at the order cancellation. Liu (2009) finds that 70% of limit orders are cancelled before being executed on NYSE. Hasbrouck and Saar (2009) investigate one hundred NASDAQ listed stocks traded on INET, showing empirical evidences that one third of the limit orders are cancelled within two seconds, which they call "fleeting orders." Liu (2009) develops a model considering the trade-off between the monitor cost and the picked-off risk. He proves that the order cancellation/revision rate is positively related to the picked off cost and non-execution cost. The picked off cost arises when the limit order price becomes stale. Non-execution cost is the cost of not taking advantage of picking off the other stale limit orders. Intuitively, investors can widen the spread to protect themselves from these two costs. So the larger the spread, the smaller the costs. Empirically, larger spread is related with less order revision. Liu (2009) notices that his prediction of negative spread revision relation is in contrast with Ellul et al.'s (2007) argument. The latter argues that there will be more order revision when the spread is larger because the investors are trying to place orders inside the spread to get higher probability of being executed. Furthermore, as an important component of the monitoring costs, the cost of extracting information is negatively related to order revision. So Liu (2009) hypothesizes that the larger stocks have more order revisions because the cost of collecting information is low for larger stocks.

Chung et al. (2008) study the speed at which the spread and the depth adjust to their equilibrium level. They first estimate the partial adjustment speed, then regress the adjustment speed on adverse selection component of the bid ask spread, PIN, price impact, size, number of trades, share price, return volatility, and institutional holding. The adjustment speed is negatively related to size and insignificantly related to institutional holding, and positively related to other

3 The other risk is non-execution risk, which the above models have thoroughly discussed.

variables. They explain their results as that market makers adjust quicker when facing larger risk and more competition.

The price aggressiveness was first defined by Biais et al. (1995), and is also used by Ranaldo (2004). Ranaldo's (2004) major conclusions are as follows. First, thicker depth on the same side encourages price aggressiveness, i.e., more market orders; and thicker depth on the opposite side discourages price aggressiveness, i.e., more limit orders. Second, transient volatility and a wider spread encourage limit orders, and discourage market orders.

4.4 Limit order patterns

On the theoretical side, Parlour (1998) predicts negative serial correlation in limit order type, because a limit buy (sell) order makes it less attractive to submit another limit buy (sell) order. Kaniel and Liu (2006) predict that limit orders are serially uncorrelated, because the market maker, after observing the order flow, sets the bid and asks the price so that future buy and sell orders are equally likely. If the orders are positively serially correlated, it is also known that the investors are employing a "follow-on" strategy. Biais et al. (1995) propose three reasons for the follow-on strategy or the positive correlation of the order types. First, split orders may induce positive order autocorrelation. Second, investors imitate order flows if they believe the orders come from informed investors. Third, investors receiving the same signal at different points of time over a period may place orders in the same direction over time. Yeo (2006) argues that if a limit order submitter undercuts the current limit orders to get price priority, it induces positive autocorrelation. Notice that Yeo's (2006) argument is related to the discussion of market resiliency. See Ellul et al. (2007, p. 638) for a review on this topic.

Ellul et al. (2007) show that there's positive autocorrelation in order types, and as quoted depth increases, limit order submitters are more likely to undercut the current quotes to get the price priority. Ranaldo (2004) also discusses depth. One thing that concerns me is that prior studies look at order by order data. They assume that every order is instantly revealed to all market participants when it is submitted or executed. It may not be the case for technical reasons, especially when the trade is very active. Ellul et al. (2007) analyze at both order by order and aggregated levels.

For the shape of the limit order book, see Roşu (2009, p. 4623), Biais et al. (1995), and Bouchaud et al. (2002). They show that the limit order book is typically "hump-shaped." That is, the limit orders cluster around some points above (below) the best ask (bid) price.

For the intraday pattern of limit orders, see Ellul et al. (2007, pp. 640–641) for the discussion of potential explanations for the intraday patterns, and also notice the "deadline effect." Ellul et al. (2007) show that limit orders are more likely and market orders are less likely late in the trading day. Ranaldo (2004, pp. 56–57) discusses some intraday patterns on the Swiss Stock Exchange.

Chapter 5
Depicting investors

In essence, how investors trade underlies every finance theory. This chapter tries to collect all the depictions of investors' trading patterns. To this end, we first need to reduce the universe of investors to several representatives.

5.1 Theory based investor taxonomy

To understand investors' trading behavior both empirically and theoretically, we need first to list the dimensions of the behavior. Keim and Madhavan (1995) in Section 2 outline several questions that are interesting and important: (a) the motivation for trade; (b) trade duration and order breakup; and (c) the choice of order type.

Firstly, the motivation for trade. To trade is to adjust the portfolio position. A major reason for adjusting portfolio is the arrival of new information. If this is the reason for "active" portfolio adjusting, there are also reasons for "passive" ones. Index funds trade mainly because of the change in index composition. Technical traders follow the patterns revealed by previous returns. Mutual funds may trade due to the cash inflow or outflow, and also due to window dressing.

Secondly, trade duration and order breakup. This dimension assumes that the desired portfolio adjustment can't be executed instantaneously. And to the extent that there's always price impact opposite to the direction of desired portfolio adjustment, traders must work out the optimal order size to maximize the total trading profits. Specific for the institutional investors, who often change positions of large quantity, they have to fragment the orders. So the desired portfolio adjustment takes time. Specifically, if the price impact is large, traders may find it optimal to trade slowly. In other words, the portfolio adjustment takes a longer time in a thinner market.

Thirdly, the choice of order type. What drives investors' strategic decision of using market versus limit orders? If the private information is short lived, the informed investor will value immediate execution more than a better price. If the longevity of information is not a concern, the so-called patience coefficient will play a key role.

5.1.1 *Informed investors*

Do informed traders trade in large or small quantities? See Chakravarty (2001) for stealth trading. Barclay and Warner (1993) are seminal works in this area. Chakravarty (2001) shows that price change is mainly associated with medium-size institution-initiated trades.

Menkhoff and Schmeling (2010) find that trades with large price impacts have the following characteristics. They argue these are the characteristics of informed traders. Anand et al. (2011, p. 198) and Linnainmaa and Saar (2012) argue that informed traders do not randomize their brokers to hide their private information. However, Cao et al. (2004) provide interesting evidences on the informed trading. They show that there are large body of insiders entering the market when their IPO lockup period expires. Their trading increases volume and share price. But interestingly, they do not impair market liquidity.

5.1.2 *Liquidity investors, noise investors, and speculators*

There are several views on the role of noise trader. Some argue that noise traders introduce speculative trading and generate additional risks for the arbitrageurs, e.g., Scheinkman and Xiong (2003), Shleifer and Vishny (1997), and Shleifer and Summers (1990). Some believe that noise traders may enhance price discovery, e.g., Harris and Schultz (1998) and Battalio et al. (1997). Noise trader and liquidity trader are often used interchangeably. However, they may have different emphasis in the literature. The liquidity trader trades only according to his exogenous liquidity need. In this vein, sometimes noise trading further refers to the trading due to the hedging needs. This interpretation of noise trading emphasizes the rational aspect of this notion. In contrast, the behavioral literature often uses noise trading to emphasize the irrational aspect. That is, it refers to the trading motivated by reasons other than the stock's fundamental information or other optimal portfolio choices. These two emphases have one thing in common: noise traders are uninformed. So difference of the emphases amounts to their trading when they have no information. Notice that uninformed does not necessarily mean irrational. Rather, uninformed investors could infer the private information of the informed trader, if the former have sufficient skills, as shown in Hong and Stein (1999) and Harris and Schultz (1998). Or uninformed investors could just provide liquidity to the market. This is the traditional role of market makers. In this role, uninformed noise traders are not liquidity traders. Or uninformed investors just irrationally trade or trade following some strategies.

Bloomfield et al. (2009) use an experiment to show the effect of noise trading on various market aspects. In their experiment, there are three types of investors: informed traders, liquidity traders, and uninformed traders. They use the uninformed traders to represent noise traders. They show that uninformed traders increase volume, provide liquidity, follow contrarian strategy, and consistent lose money. When the stock price deviates extremely from the true fundamental value, uninformed trading harms price discovery. So as Bloomfield et al. (2009, p. 2278) suggest: "research considering the behavior of noise traders needs to distinguish clearly between liquidity traders, who trade for consumption and risk sharing and, hence, have rational liquidity needs, and 'pure' uninformed traders, who trade without information on their own volition and end up with creating excess noise in the market."

Another important role of noise traders is to maintain a liquid market, as argued by Black (1986), among others. In this view, noise traders "lose money on average, and hence, resolve the Grossman-Stiglitz conundrum of how informed trading is compensated in an informationally efficient market (Bloomfield et al., 2009, p.2277)."

The noise trader is, relative to the informed trader, in a disadvantageous position. It is natural to believe that the noise trader is losing money to his informed counterparty. Furthermore, in the long run, the noise trader will lose all his money and be driven out of the market. This is a crucial assumption for traditional asset pricing theory, that is, the noise trader does not affect the asset price in the long run, so the asset pricing that discusses the long run asset return can safely ignore the effect of noise traders. De Long et al. (1990b) show that this is not necessarily the case. They prove that the noise traders exert effect on asset prices. Oberlechner and Osler (2012, pp. 94–95) show that overconfident foreign currency dealers do survive; see their work for reasons why irrational investors should or should not be driven out of the market. Kyle and Wang (1997) and Wang (2001) provide theoretical reasons why they are not driven out; see also Hirshleifer and Luo (2001).

However, Blume and Easley (2006) and Sandroni (2000) show that markets favor rational investors, implying that irrational investors will be driven out of the market eventually. Seru et al. (2010) show empirical evidence that some individual investors do cease to trade after they realize that they consistently lose money.

5.2 Identity based investor taxonomy

5.2.1 Individual investors

Individual investors, or household investors, are found to pursue contrarian strategies: Grinblatt and Keloharju (2001b), Grinblatt and Keloharju (2000) for household investors; Odean (1998a), Griffin et al. (2003) for investors of the brokerage houses that are supposed to specializing in catering to the individual investors.

Linnainmaa (2010) summarizes four characteristics of individual investors that prior literature has found: misinterpretation of new information, poor stock-picking skills, the disposition effect, and contrarian trading strategies. Linnainmaa (2010) shows that individual investors predominately use limit orders, and they tend to ignore the orders after they place them. Griffin et al. (2003) use daily and intradaily data to show the relation between institutional and individual trading and the stock return. See my discussion in the subsection of institutional investors.

Grinblatt and Keloharju (2001b) conduct a thorough analysis on the trading behavior in Finland. They show that "past returns, reference price effects, the size of the holding period capital gain or loss, tax-loss selling, and, to a small extent, the smoothing of consumption over the life cycle all are determinants of trading" (p. 614). They find disposition effect for all the investors. But "sophisticated investor classes place less weight on past returns in deciding whether the trade is to be a buy or sell." Domestic investors, which tend to be less sophisticated, are contrarians, and foreign investors are momentum investors. Investors tend to sell when they are young and old, they buy stocks in middle age.

Vissing-Jorgensen (2003) analyzes the UBS/Gallup survey data on individual investors' expectation on stock return along with a number of investor characteristics. The author finds that "expected returns were high at the peak of the market." Traditional finance theory suggests that the expected returns should be low when the stock price is high. So this evidence is consistent with the view that investors do have behavioral bias. Moreover, "investors' beliefs depend on their own investment experience (a version of the law of small numbers; the dependence of beliefs on own past portfolio performance is asymmetric, consistent with theories of biased self-attribution)." Individual investors with sophistication also exhibit these biases, but to a lesser degree.

Coval et al. (2005) study the accounts of a brokerage house. They show that there exists a group of investors who can persistently outperform the other group of investors. This evidence indicates that "skillful individual investors exploit market inefficiencies to earn abnormal profits, above and beyond any profits available from well-known strategies based upon size, value, or momentum."

Dorn et al. (2008) illustrate retail clients of a German brokerage firm. Feng and Seasholes (2004) illustrate retail clients of a Chinese brokerage firm. Both studies show that individual investors' trading is correlated.

Other studies of retail investors include Kumar and Lee (2006), Barber et al. (2009), and Brown et al. (2008).

5.2.2 Institutional investors

A large body of literature finds empirical evidence that institutional investors pursue momentum strategies: Grinblatt et al. (1995) for mutual fund managers; Badrinath and Wahal (2002) for general institutional investors; and Brennan and Cao (1997), Choe et al. (1999), Grinblatt and Keloharju (2000), Froot et al. (2001), Grinblatt and Keloharju (2001b), and Richards (2005) for foreign investors. See Sias et al. (2006), especially for the discussion on the holding changes versus number of institutional shareholders. Sias and Starks (1997) show institutional investors trading are persistent in their daily trading patterns. Griffin et al. (2003) show that institutional investors buy (sell) stocks following past positive (negative) returns, but individual investors respond to past return in the opposite way. Their finding implies that institutional and individual investors receive or interpret information differently, and each group is the counterparty of the other. Moreover, the authors find a strong contemporaneous positive (negative) relation between institutional (individual) trading and daily stock returns. They find little evidence that institutional or individual trading predict future stock returns. Griffin et al.'s (2003) evidence are more convincing because they use daily and intradaily data.

Grinblatt and Keloharju (2001b) provide detailed discussion on various investor groups. See the discussions in the subsection of individual investors. Grinblatt and Keloharju (2001a) show that the firm's language, culture, and distance from the investor affect the investor's choice. But "the influence of distance, language, and culture on stockholdings and trades is generally smaller for financially savvy institutions than for households or less savvy institutions" (p. 1054).

Gompers and Metrick (2001) show that "large" institutional investors prefer large stocks. When the large institutional investors increase their shares in stock market, prices of large stocks increase. And part of the disappearance of small stock premium can be attributed to the increase in large institutional investors.

Falkenstein (1996) document that mutual funds prefer the stocks with 1) high visibility, 2) low transaction costs, and 3) high idiosyncratic volatility. The authors conjecture that mutual funds may have some comparative advantage of holding these stocks. The "over-weight" on these stocks are due to frictions. However, Bennett et al. (2003) provide empirical evidence that institutions' preference has shifted to smaller stocks. Choi and Sias (2009) document that institutional investors do herd in and out particular industries. The reason to "industry herding" could be correlated signals or style investing.

5.2.3 Foreign investors

To the extent that investors exhibit home bias, and culture and language difference create barriers for foreign investors, foreign investors are a meaningful group to be studied.

Richards (2005) uses data on six emerging markets and documents that foreign investors are following positive feedback trading to both the mature and domestic market returns. These foreign investors have large price impact on the domestic markets. Grinblatt and Keloharju (2001b) provide detailed discussion on various investor groups. See the discussions in the subsection of individual investors.

Brennan and Cao (1997) "present a theoretical model and empirical evidence that supports the view that foreign investors should pursue momentum strategies and achieve inferior performance because they are less informed than domestic investors." But Grinblatt and Keloharju (2000) show that foreign investors in the Finnish market achieve superior performance, and this superior performance is not driven by their momentum strategies. Choe et al. (1999) and Froot et al. (2001) also find that foreign investors follow momentum strategies.

5.3 Investor sophistication

5.3.1 What does sophistication mean?

According to Tirole (2011, p. 301):

> It is often assumed that more information (increased transparency) reduces the competitive advantage that sophisticated investors have over unsophisticated ones. This reasoning is correct if what differentiates sophisticated investors is the ability to go and collect facts. It is flawed if sophistication refers to a higher ability to figure out what a given information actually means (Pagano and Volpin, 2010). Thus if what is at stake is the differential ability to process information, more public information means higher asymmetries of information and therefore more concern for unsophisticated buyers.

Dang et al. (2010) suggest that when there is little doubt about the quality of the debt claims, the market is liquid and less concerned about the adverse selection problem. However, when bad news comes and therefore the market becomes doubtful about the quality of debt, an adverse selection problem emerges. In this sense, bad news not only brings down the debt price, but also intrigue adverse selection concerns and thus an illiquid market. This idea is summarized by Tirole (2011, p. 303). See also Malherbe (2011), who distinguishes "liquidity-driven" versus "information driven" sellers.

5.3.2 The effect of investor sophistication

Vissing-Jorgensen (2003) show that sophistication makes individual investors less prone to the behavioral biases.

Haruvy et al. (2007) use an experiment to study how investors form expectation. Their experiment settings generate both bubbles and crashes, and the stock value is set to converge to its fundamental value eventually. They find that investors form expectations from both prior and current market state: "[A]s traders gain experience, market bubbles shrink and prices track fundamentals more closely" (p. 1917). In addition, the authors also find that "as long as prices deviate from fundamental values, data on individual traders' expectations can be useful to an observer in predicting future price movements" (p. 1919).

5.4 Herding and correlated trading

5.4.1 Empirical evidence

On the empirical side, many investor classes exhibit correlated trading, also known as herding. Lakonishok et al. (1992), Wermers (1999), and Wylie (2005) show that institutional investors, fund managers, for example, herd. Barber et al. (2006), Kumar and Lee (2006), and Dorn et al. (2008) document that retail investors also herd. Dorn et al. (2008) also indicate that retail investors herd even stronger than institutional investors.

Lakonishok et al. (1992) propose the canonical method to measure herding. Lakonishok et al.'s (1992) methodology treats sells similarly as buys. This treatment is implausible when short selling is constrained. Wylie (2005) proposes a new measure to account for this potential bias.

If investors, or a substantial group of investors, systematically trade toward the on direction, this herding may affect price formation. Griffin et al. (2003) show that institutional (individual) trading follows past returns in the same (opposite) direction. See my discussion in the subsection of institutional investors.

5.4.2 Theoretical explanations

On the theoretical side, Colla and Mele (2010) propose a model in which investors have heterogeneous information endowments. Some investors' information are more closely correlated than other groups. They show that correlation decreases over time, and eventually the correlation is negative for relatively distant investors.

Why do investors herd? The researchers have proposed the following explanations. Devenow and Welch (1996) provide an excellent summary:

1. Wylie (2005) argues that short selling constraint may be a reason.

2. Dorn et al. (2008) and Linnainmaa (2010) argue that retail investors' usage of limit orders can be a reason: "A price jump can trigger the execution of limit sell orders that were submitted days or even weeks apart" (Dorn et al., 2008, p. 886).

3. Dorn et al. (2008) discuss other reasons: the correlated timing for nonspeculative trading (for example, at pay days). But Dorn et al. (2008) also find that speculative trading, which is presumably driven by information, is even strongly correlated.

4. Investors may receive correlated signals, or interpret the signals similarly. And if investors receive and interpret signals sequentially, their trading should be correlated both cross sectionally and sequentially. The proximity of investors may be one reason for the correlated signals.

5. Investors might be attracted by the same groups of stocks, for example, style investing (Barberis and Shleifer, 2003). Falkenstein (1996) shows empirical evidence that mutual funds prefer certain kind of stocks. The authors conjecture that this preference may be due to some friction, but not for informational or reputation reasons. Bennett et al. (2003) find a shift of institutional investors' preference from large stocks to small stocks. Choi and Sias (2009) document evidence of industry herding.

6. Hirshleifer et al. (1994) provide a model in which some investors obtain information earlier than others. Therefore, the sequential information prompts investors to behave like herding. Moreover, the earlier informed investors' expected utility increases with the number of later informed investors. There are multi equilibria and investors may also herd on certain stocks, while ignoring other stocks.

7. Keynes's (1936) beauty contest is a good explanation for herding. In this beauty contest explanation, the absolute beauty does not matter. What matters is what other people think. Similarly, in stock markets, a stock's true value does not matter. What matters is at what price other traders think it should be. Froot et al. (1992) provide a similar model in which short-horizon traders allocate their research efforts on the aspects that every other trader cares. And these aspects do not necessarily reflect a stock's fundamental value. This allocation of research efforts lead to herding. Banerjee (1992) provides a similar model.

8. Reputation is a reason for herding. According to Keynes (1936, p. 158): "Worldly wisdom teaches that it is better for reputation to fail conventionally

than to succeed unconventionally." Scharfstein and Stein (1990) provide a model on this explanation; see also Zwiebel (1995).

9. One implication of herding is that traders put too many weights on the signals conveyed by other traders' actions, while putting too few weights on their own signals. The more extreme case could be that herding traders ignore their own signals. Bikhchandani et al. (1992) provide a rational model that explains why it is optimal to ignore their own signals. When the traders act sequentially, the subsequent traders observe the earlier traders' actions and infer their private signals. When these observations accumulate to a certain point, the weight of their own private signals would be too small, thus ignoring their own signals becomes optimal.

10. Devenow and Welch (1996, p. 605) summarize the rational herding literature into three lines of explanations: 1) payoff externality of adopting the same actions as other agents, for example, bank runs; 2) uncertainty on agents' ability leads them to optimally hide in the herd (Scharfstein and Stein, 1990; Zwiebel, 1995); 3) informational cascades models show that agents optimally ignore their own signals after observing enough number of prior actions (Banerjee, 1992; Froot et al., 1992).

11. Demarzo et al. (2004) develop a model in which part of the agents' consumptions are tied up with local resources. Therefore, the agents' portfolio choices are correlated with other community members, thus leading to herding.

5.5 Trading behavior

5.5.1 Trading and contemporaneous returns

Wermers (1999) and Nofsinger and Sias (1999) show strong evidence that institutional buying is positively related with contemporaneous returns at a quarterly and annual basis. Griffin et al. (2003) provide daily and intradaily evidence reinforcing this contemporaneous relations.

Haruvy et al. (2007) use an experiment to show that investors form expectation on future price movements based on past market trends and current market state. Moreover, investors' expectations do affect their trading. Their evidence provide some insight into the relation between trading and past returns.

5.5.2 *Trading horizon*

Froot et al. (1992, p. 1461) cite a foreign exchange trader as saying: "Ninety percent of what we do is based on perception. It doesn't matter if that perception is right or wrong or real. It only matters that other people in the market believe it. I may know it's crazy, I may think it's wrong. But I lose my shirt by ignoring it. This business turns on decisions made in seconds. If you wait a minute to reflect on things, you're lost. I can't afford to be five steps ahead of everybody else in the market. That's suicide." It seems that many traders, even professional traders, have short investment horizons.

Besides the fancy economic models, there are several reasons why traders prefer short investment horizons: 1) to show their skills; 2) if the money is tied up in long-horizon investments, there would be opportunity costs when better investment opportunities arise in the future (see footnote 2 in Froot et al., 1992, p. 1462).

Froot et al. (1992) provide a sharp insight compared to the conventional asset pricing models. That is, information spillover is positive if traders have short investment horizons, because they can make a profit on their private information only if other traders also know the information, albeit a bit later, when the first group unwind their positions. In contrast, when all traders have long investment horizons, which means that the stock's true value will eventually reveal itself, information spillover is negative.

5.5.3 *Value investing*

Bhattacharya and Galpin (2011) propose a metric gauging the popularity of value-weighting. By value-weighting, they mean the value weighted (market) portfolios. Mean variance efficient portfolio theory suggests that investors should hold value weighted market portfolios and risk-free assets. Furthermore, the authors show that if every investor chooses portfolios in the way suggested by the portfolio theory, then the dollar turnover, defined as dollar volume traded divided by the market cap of the stock, should be identical for all stocks (see Bhattacharya and Galpin, 2011, p. 741). The more popular the value-weighted portfolio, the more likely investors are to follow the instruction of the portfolio theory, and the less likely they are to do value investing. Bhattacharya and Galpin (2011) show that value investing is more popular in an emerging market, because better information environment lowers the profitability of informed trading.[1]

Bhattacharya and Galpin (2011, p. 740) suggest that Cremers and Petajisto (2009) and Petajisto (2009) show the existence of stock picking or signs of value investing.

1 China is an emerging market, but is more dominated by value investing (see Table 1, Bhattacharya and Galpin, 2011, p. 745).

Chapter 6
Mutual funds

6.1 Fund performance and fund manager skills

6.1.1 Overview of fund manager skills

A key service that mutual funds provide is creating value for the fundholders.

Do the funds achieve this goal? Although having been examined ever since Jensen (1968), this question has no definite answers. In the literature, this question has been rephrased as: can the funds systematically outperform the market? Or do fund managers have superior skills? As observed by Wermers (2000), there are two approaches to examine these questions: return-based and holding-based approaches. A return-based approach examines whether the funds earn higher return. If they do, the fund managers have superior skills. A holding-based approach examines whether fund managers can pick up outperforming stocks.

Let us first look at the return-based approach. This approach evaluates risk adjusted fund returns, usually after-fee returns. Goetzmann et al. (2007) and Ferson (2010) review the measures. Strikingly, few funds have a positive alpha, showing that fund managers have no superior skills. And there are further attacks on fund manager skills. Obviously, beating the market for a few times does not imply a superior skill. In other words, we not only look at the fund performance, but also the persistence of the performance. Fund performances persistence is well documented, but not well explained, observed by Carhart (1997). A stylized fact seems to be that fund outperformance persists in the short run, and reverses in the long run, whereas underperformance persists in both the short and long run. The outperformance persistence in the short run is also called the "hot hand" phenomenon. Hendricks et al. (1993), Goetzmann and Ibbotson (1994), and Brown and Goetzmann (1995) document empirical evidences of the hot hand. In the long run, outperformance reverses, which rejects superior skills. Carhart (1997) documents this reversion. Interestingly, Grinblatt and Titman (1992), Elton et al. (1996a), and Elton et al. (1996b) show long-term performance persistence and attribute this to fund managers' stock-picking talents. Carhart (1997) further argue that the more the fund trade, the higher the transaction cost, and furthermore, the lower the return is. This argument imposes another attack on fund manager skills.

The holding-based approach investigates whether fund managers can pick out outperforming stocks. Wermers (2006) surveys the studies using holding data. Cohen et al. (2005) differ from the traditional holding-based approach studies. They show that if a fund holds a lot of stocks which are also held by the majority of the fund industry, this fund outperforms.

A recent trend in explaining and detecting fund manager skills is to look at the "activeness" of the portfolios. If a fund manager exhibits more "selectivity," that is, more deviation from the benchmark, then she is more likely to have skill. See Amihud and Goyenko (2013, p. 668) for studies on this issue.

6.1.2 Factors affecting fund performance

Brown and Goetzmann (2003, 1997) define the methods to classify fund styles. Sun et al. (2012, p. 99) contend that "this statistical approach precludes possible misclassification of fund styles due to strategic self-reporting, [and it] also allows for time-varying grouping, as some funds may change investment strategies over time." Sun et al. (2012) document that hedge funds with more unique trading strategies outperform the funds using public known strategies.

Given the mixed evidence on fund manager skills, some studies try to find what affects fund performance, assuming no explicit roles of fund manager skills. Perold and Jr. Salomon (1991), Edelen (1999) and Indro et al. (1999) show a negative relationship between fund size and fund performances; see also Zheng (1999) and Chen et al. (2004). Zhao (2004) shows that funds are closed because of the spill-over effect. Then what drives the negative relationship between fund size and performance? Firstly, when the fund size exceeds some critical point, the economy of scale disappears, and the cost increases with fund size. Chan et al. (2002) discuss the fund style in a framework of two dimensions: size (defined as the stock's market capitalization) and value-growth (defined as the book-to-market ratio).

6.2 Funds herding

Choi and Sias (2009, p. 472) summarize six possible reasons for institutional herding. They show evidence that institutions herd in industries, and their evidence is consistent with the correlated signal explanation. As they observe, there are two ways of measuring the herding.

Scharfstein and Stein (1990) argue that managers will mimic the decisions of other managers. This herding behavior is rational in the views of managers. This herding behavior is due to managers' concern about their reputation in the labor market. That is, it hurts the manager's reputation to be "lone fools," and "there would be comfort in numbers" if things go wrong. In this setting, managers will pay more attention to what other managers do, instead of their own private signals. Of course, these happen in the market with asymmetric information on manager's skills. Zwiebel (1995) discusses similar ideas.

In Scharfstein and Stein's (1990) model, "managers who care only about their reputation will always herd but managers who care about profits will have to trade off the loss of reputation against profits" (from Dass et al., 2008, p. 52). Dass et al. (2008) explore this trade off using the data around the 2000 market bubble. They show that high incentive contracts will induce managers to invest less on bubble stocks, or put differently, will lead managers to less herding. Their findings cast new lights on the "limit of arbitrage" literature.

Empirical evidences on mutual fund herding can be found in Wermers (1999), Grinblatt et al. (1995), and Sias (2004).

As for the effect of institutional herding on the stock prices, the current empirical evidence is mixed. Dasgupta et al. (2011, p. 892) comment: "Studies examining the short-term impact of institutional trading generally find that herding has a stabilizing effect on prices. In contrast, studies focusing on longer horizons often find that herding predicts reversals in returns, thus providing empirical evidence in favor of Trichet's view (that is, destabilizing the market)."

Dasgupta et al. (2011) develop a model in which market makers charge higher prices for the stocks that institutions herd in, therefore predicting a lower return in the future. This model provides an explanation for the long term price reversal following an institutional herding.

6.3 Incentives and the risk shifting

One problem is to set the optimal contract. The other problem is how the contract affects investing. When investigating the optimal contract, researchers are concerned with the agency costs borne by the investors. The optimal contract should entice the fund managers to choose optimal portfolio (and risk), and entice them to exert the best effort. Massa and Patgiri (2009, p. 1777) summarizes these two themes of optimal contract in the following way, although they do not intend to answer this theoretical question: "Agency theory claims that investors can alleviate some agency problems through high-incentive contracts for managers. Such contracts would mean that managers' payoffs were more closely related to their performance, which could increase managers' efforts and thus lead to better performance. At the same time, high-incentive contracts would also induce managers to take more risks." For a study that discusses the optimal contract, refer to Dybvig et al. (2010).

As for the effects of contract on fund performance, one line of inquiry discusses the risk-taking shift under specific contract. The other line investigates empirically: which type of contract "generates" higher return? Both lines assume the contract as given. Non-linear performance-flow relationship is a call option in terms of fund managers' compensation (Sirri and Tufano, 1998). This relation affects fund managers' risk-taking behavior; see Chevalier and Ellison (1997), Brown et al. (1996), Busse (2001), Goriaev et al. (2005), Chen and Pennacchi (2009). These studies are "tournament" researches. Notice that fund managers may alter two kinds of riskiness of the fund's portfolios: standard deviation of the "track errors" and of the returns (Chen and Pennacchi, 2009).

Massa and Patgiri (2009) investigate empirically whether high-incentive funds deliver higher performance. Their motivation is that high-incentive, on the one hand, align the interests of investors and managers better, while on the other hand, it encourages managers to take more risks. They want to investigate which effect dominates. They find managers do take more risks, but they can deliver more superior performance.

Elton et al. (2003) study the incentive fees. The incentive fees scheme, to some extent, alters the incentives of the fund managers. With fixed fees, fund managers are encouraged to expand the size of funds under management. With incentive fees, fund managers are aligned with that of the investors.

What spoils the financial industry? By spoil, I mean the distorted incentive scheme, which results in aggressive risk-taking. The answer is simple, when the game is such that you have little to lose, while a lot to win, you are surely aggressive. Brown et al. (1996) argue that the fund industry is inherently of tournament nature. Thus interim losers will increase the risk level of their fund to try to fill the "deficit." Aware of what their interim loser competitors will do, interim winners will also increase the risk level, but to a lower extent. Furthermore, size and age negatively affect this risk level adjustment, which predicts that new funds and small funds will act more progressively when increasing risk level. A list of related literatures (cited from Chen and Pennacchi, 2009) includes:

1. Grinblatt and Titman (1993) show how compensation contracts that include a bonus for good performance can produce moral hazard incentives.
2. Starks (1987) considers the moral hazard incentives of a bonus contract, focusing on situations of asymmetric information between investors and fund managers.
3. Das and Sundaram (2002)
4. Dybvig et al. (2010)
5. Huberman and Kandel (1993), Heinkel and Stoughton (1994), and Huddart (1999)
6. Carpenter (2000), Cuoco and Kaniel (2011), and Basak et al. (2007)
7. Chevalier and Ellison (1997)
8. BHS (1996)
9. Koski and Pontiff (1999)
10. Busse (2001)
11. GNW (2005)

6.4 Fund flow and investor's preferences

6.4.1 Flow-performance relationship

Calvet et al. (2009) show that individual investors do not redeem immediately after the funds lose money. Due to the non-linear performance-flow relationship, fund managers are granted a call option, in the sense that if a remarkably high return is achieved, a large amount of funds will be poured into their fund; while if a modest or even poor return is achieved, relatively less funds will withdraw. Brown et al. (1996) and Chevalier and Ellison (1997) explicitly discussed this topic and have shown that fund managers increase the volatility of their fund to maximize the value of this call option, especially during the latter part of the calendar year.

Li et al. (2011) and Ding et al. (2011) demonstrate that the flow-performance relation is concave in hedge funds, while this relation in mutual funds are convex. See also Ippolito (1992), Gruber (1996), Sirri and Tufano (1998), Goetzmann and Peles (1997), Del Guercio and Tkac (2002), Cao et al. (2008), Capon et al. (1996), and Berk and Green (2004).

6.4.2 Explanations for asymmetric performance-flow relationship

Lynch and Musto (2003) explicitly take into account the replacement of fund manager and stock-picking algorithm. Since the investor's delegation of his money to fund implies delegation of choosing the "right" fund manager and choosing the "right" stock-picking algorithm, investors may reasonably expect that badly performing fund managers in the current period may be replaced by other fund managers, or they may choose a different stock-picking algorithm. So why bother withdrawing their money from the badly performing funds? Wilcox (2003) discusses the investor preferences using an experiment. For the non-linear performance-flow relationship, see Sirri and Tufano (1998, p. 1595) for a list of papers on that topic.

6.4.3 Investor's purchasing process

As protested by Capon et al. (1996), classical analysis of investors' investing decision making process assumes, to a large extent wrongly, that they care only about risk and return, the two factors which form the cornerstones of modern finance theory. Leading on from this, Goetzmann and Ibbotson (1994) coined a term "naive investors." Capon et al. (1996) use survey data to show that a large portion of mutual fund investors are "naive investors" who care rarely about the risk or return and are almost driven by advisors' advices or advertisements, and quite a few investors have no idea about the investment styles and areas of the funds they invest in. Another important and interesting fact is that most investors concentrate their investments within one fund family. The critical message of the survey is that most investors are concerned about more than risk and return.

Authors who have researched this topic include: Capon et al. (1996), Goetzmann and Peles (1997), Goetzmann and Ibbotson (1994), Barber and Odean (2008), Barber et al. (2005), Berk and Green (2004), and Wilcox (2003)

6.4.4 Advertising

Bergstresser et al. (2009) show that broker-sold funds do not deliver better performance. Boldin and Cici (2010) show evidence that some index fund investors, who are supposed to be more likely to make rational choices, are actually investing in sub-optimal funds, and attribute this irrationality to the broker's marketing efforts. Notably Choi et al. (2010) also investigate the individual investors' suboptimal choice of index funds. As index funds try to mimic index returns, there is little difference among the funds, except the fees. So the optimal choice should be the funds charging lowest fees. In Choi et al.'s (2010) experiment, the subjects systematically violate the optimal choice. Their evidence shows that the suboptimal choice is mainly due to financial literacy.

6.4.5 Smart or dumb money effect

Smart money effect was first found by Gruber (1996), followed by Zheng (1999). Sapp and Tiwari (2004) argue that the smart money effect is mainly driven by momentum effects. Keswani and Stolin (2008) provide evidence of smart money effect using more detailed British data. They also contend that Sapp and Tiwari's (2004) conclusion is due to their emphasis on the pre-1991 period.

Frazzini and Lamont (2008) argues the smart money effect exists, if it does, only in the short horizon. In the long run, dumb money effect dominates. Rakowski and Wang (2009) document evidence that investors are more consistent with contrarian in short term, and momentum in the long term. They ask the question: is the fund flow mean reverting or reversal, and is the investor contrarian or momentum?

6.5 Fund fees

Nanda et al. (2000) discuss the load and non-load types of funds. They argue load acts as a screening mechanism to cater to specific clientele with specific liquidity needs. Carhart (1997) has shown that high fees can explain why some funds perform poorly. See Gil-Bazo and Ruiz-Verd (2008, p. 873) for a list of papers discussing the anomaly that higher fees predict lower return: Elton et al. (1993), Gruber (1996), Carhart (1997), Harless and Peterson (1998), Chevalier and Ellison (1999), Keswani and Stolin (2008), Das and Sundaram (2002) and Malhotra and Mcleod (1997).

Sharpe (1966) documents that the differences of mutual fund performance are attributable to level of fees. Gil-Bazo and Ruiz-Verd (2009) find a robust negative relation between before-fee risk-adjusted performance and fees. It is, to some extent, an anomaly in the sense that poor-performers are able to charge more to the investors. They conjecture several explanations. The central idea is that poor-performing funds focus on a special group of investors, which are performance-insensitive (Christoffersen and Musto, 2002) or unsophisticated (Gil-Bazo and Ruiz-Verd, 2008). So there should be little wonder that these investors are over-charged. Another explanation is that high marketing expenses give rise to the low performance. The authors also address the possibilities that stricter fund governance leads to better fee-charging.

Investors' exogenous liquidity needs usually force funds to liquidate their assets. Therefore, funds can be better off if a smaller portion of their investors redeems. In other words, investors with lower and more certain future liquidity needs are customers worthy of chasing. So loads and redemption fees can be structured in order to make the investors self-select. Chordia (1996) and Nanda et al. (2000) explore this topic.

Khorana et al. (2009) measure fund fees in the following three ways: management fees, expense ratio, and total shareholder costs (TSCs). And is there economy of scale for the management expenses? See Dermine and Röller (1992) for more detailed discussions on this.

Large funds tend to have a low expenses ratio, and funds with high expenses have a higher growth rate in size, and advertising expenses work in the sense that they attract more inflows. Also, front-end loads and commissions, which are in-your-face expenses, strongly negatively affect investors' choices, while there is no relation between flows and annual expenses (Barber et al., 2005).

Sirri and Tufano (1998) emphasize the costs for the investors to search funds.

They argue that besides the relationship between fees level, risk, performance and flows, lowering investors' searching costs (measured by fund complex size, marketing expenses, and media coverage) may attract more flows.

Two strands have been identified. One strand of research emphasizes the investors' searching processes, including Sirri and Tufano (1998) and Barber et al. (2005). They attempt to identify what factors play roles in investors' funds decisions. The other strand emphasizes the rationality of fees-settings, especially the role of loads as screening investors with different liquidity needs, such as Chordia (1996) and Nanda et al. (2000).

There is a third strand that explores the market structure of the fund industry, such as Luo (2002) and Gil-Bazo and Ruiz-Verd (2008). Two issues should be noted. Firstly, if the market is imperfect, there is rent of the advantageous market power to be extracted. Secondly, the services the fund industry provides is very special.

There has been some economic models of fee setting and investors' purchasing behavior. An important theme in this line of study is that it pays for funds to send signals about their quality. Two signals are studied in the literature: advertisements and prices. The rationality of advertising is that since investors can process only limited information and the costs of searching is high, advertisements help funds enter the "consideration set." Advertisements are mainly connected with search costs. Prices can be another means of signaling. See García and Vanden (2009) for an example.

6.6 Governance of funds

Agency problems within funds are manifold. Firstly, fund managers may not maximize fund holders' interests when making investment decisions, which has been explored by the literature on managers' incentives. Secondly, fund management firms (or called fund sponsors) may charge excessive fees to fund holders.

Chinese funds differ from their American counterparties in institutional forms. According to laws and regulations in the U.S., every fund has a board that is supposed to represent the interests of the fund holders. And this board is entitled to choose the fund sponsors, and negotiate the fees with fund sponsors. Although this mechanism is far from perfect to protect fund holders, as shown by Tufano and Sevick (1997), it provides some protection after all in comparison with that in China. In China, funds do not have their own boards. The congregation of fund holders have similar legal power to that of the fund's board in U.S. However, the fund expense ratios are set in the initialization contract, and are not negotiated on an annual basis. Therefore, in practice, the congregation of fund holders has very limited power to punish poorly performing fund sponsors, given the incredible coordination due to the large amount of the participants attending the congregation of fund holders.

The U.S. fund industry differs from China's in the respect that the former has a board elected by and representing the fund's shareholders. The board members usually have close relation with the advisory firms (fund management firms in China), because initially the latter is only a shareholder of the fund. Close relation between the board and the firm they hire may facilitate the monitoring, and may also harm shareholders' interests. Which effect dominates? Kuhnen (2009) finds that these two effects balance out.

Chapter 7
Prices of IPO and SEO

This chapter focuses on a special type of prices, namely the stock prices of initial public offering and seasoned equity offering. Ritter and Welch (2002) review the topics in this area. Ellis et al. (2000) give some descriptions of the institutional details. Notice the time trend of the activities. Ritter and Welch (2002) emphasize this point.

7.1 Why and when to issue new equities

Altı and Sulaeman (2012, p. 62) use dimensions of issuance decisions other than the probability of an issuance. These dimensions include: how quickly the firm announces the issuance once the "conditions" to issue are met, the time spent on the issuance arrangement (i.e., the time between announcement and the offer), the amount of proceeds in the offer.

Firms go to public only when they grow and mature. But why? Chemmanur and Fulghieri (1999) provide a trade-off between going public versus staying private. Venture capitalists can't diversify their holding, so they offer a lower price to the entrepreneur than an outsider body of investors. However, outsider investors have difficulty with finding the true value of the firm. This is the trade-off.

Prior literature has found significant evidence of "Clustering of Issuing" (Bayless and Chaplinsky, 1996; Choe et al., 1993; Loughran and Ritter, 1997; Spiess and Affleck-Graves, 1995; Kim and Weisbach, 2008). Baker and Wurgler (2002) do not directly discuss SEO, but this is a prominent paper, or seminal paper on market timing hypothesis. Chandra and Nayar (2008) discuss the long-run underperformance following the private placed debt. They contend that the reason is because the management chooses to issue debt prior to the bad news being known to the public, namely that the management manipulates the information flow to the market. Pástor and Veronesi (2005) provide a broader version of market timing model, where firms choose optimal timing to go public. The market conditions are modeled in three dimensions: expected market return, aggregate profitability, and prior price uncertainty.

DeAngelo et al. (2010) argue that although the market timing is a good explanation, it is not of first order importance in determining the issue decisions: "The primary reason that firms conduct SEOs is to meet a near-term need for cash (p. 276)." They propose the following counter-arguments. Firstly, not all the firms take advantage of their over-priced stock prices. Secondly, most issuers do not stockpile SEO proceeds.

Li et al. (2009) argue that the pre-offer positive abnormal return, which is usually labeled as the evidence of market timing, can be well explained by the cyclical of return and investment. Pástor and Veronesi (2005) argue that the absence of empirical relation between book-to-market ratio and IPO volume indicates the behavioral story is fully supported by empirical evidences, although they do not claim the mispriced version of the behavioral story is completely wrong. Altı and Sulaeman (2012) show that the high stock returns themselves do not trigger an offering. The high stock returns combined with a strong demand from institutions trigger an offering. Institution demands can predict equity issuance because institution demands serve as a certificate of the firm value. So the market is more likely to receive the issuance, and thus it enhances the probability of a successful issuance. The authors further show that the firm's prior investment bankers help the firm to identify potential institution demands. With regard to the price movement after the SEO announcement, the authors find that issuances with high institution demands recover from the negative reaction to the announcements. Thus they show strong evidence that strong institution demand enhances the market reception of the SEO, and thus firms are more likely to issue stocks when they find a strong institution demand.

The central idea of market timing hypothesis is that firms tend to take advantage of the market mispricing. So market timing hypothesis predicts a pre-offer positive abnormal return, indicating the stock is over-valued before issues. Reinforcing this evidence, a long-term negative return can be explained by that the market corrects the mispricing gradually. Another evidence supporting market timing is the issuing firm's stockpiling of cash. Since they are simply taking advantage the opportunity window, they do not necessarily have the sufficient investments to spend all the money they raise (Kim and Weisbach, 2008), or they will invest in what they would not make otherwise (Blanchard et al., 1993; Baker et al., 2003).

7.2 Choice of issue types

This topic is broadly related to the choice of methods to finance the corporations. The financing methods form a hierarchy. On the top of this hierarchy is the choice between internal funds, debt, equity, etc. Along the lines of debt, equity, etc., there are many sub-methods to choose. For example, for debt financing, the firm can choose private placed debt, bonds, bank loans, etc. For equity financing, the firm can choose between public issue, rights offer, and private placement. Akhigbe et al. (2006) summarize the firm characteristics variables related to choice of issue type.

Cronqvist and Nilsson (2005) contend that family control is a major determinant in issue type choice, namely that family controlled firms tend to raise new equity via rights offering. Moreover, firms issue new equity to new business partners via private placement to reduce the moral hazard costs embedded in the cooperation with business partners. Asymmetric information is also found to play some roles in issue type choices.

Wruck and Wu (2009) discuss the effect of relationship on market response and the long term performance. They find that issues to investors with relationships and governance influence on the firms create values. Folta and Janney (2004) provide evidence consistent with the private placement's role of enhancing governance and mitigating asymmetric information, so that the long term return on private placement is higher.

7.3 New issuance pricing

Underwriters typically allocate more shares than that are issued. This mechanism is supposed to be used to stabilize the after issuance market. Bartling and Park (2010) discusses how this mechanism affects IPO pricing. Liu and Ritter (2011) argue that issuing firms care about non-pricing dimensions of the IPO, and the underwriters have differentiating expertise, so the IPO market is not competitive, therefore issuing firms are willing to accept underpricing. That is, IPO proceeds are not the sole aim of the issuing firms.

Bookbuilding and allocation is a line of inquiry that attracts increasing attention. Benveniste and Spindt (1989) is the seminal example of such. Hanley (1993) documents the offer price revision and underpricing. Goldstein et al. (2011) show that institutional investors pay lead underwriters abnormal commissions to obtain favorable IPO allocations.

Explanations for discounts for privately placed SEO include:

1. Compensations for the expected monitoring service and expert advice (Wruck, 1989);
2. Illiquidity (Silber, 1991);
3. Information production (Hertzel and Smith, 1993);
4. Private investors' "true" assessment of the firm values (Hertzel et al., 2002).

As for the empirical results, there are two terms related to SEO pricing: discount and underpricing. The former is defined as the return from the preannouncement closing price to the offer price. The latter is defined as the return from the first post-offer trading day closing price to the offer price. However, Corwin (2003) does not use these terms exactly.

7.4 Trading around IPO and SEO

Due to the market participant's belief of manipulative trading prior to SEO, SEC proposes Rule 10b-21 and Rule 105 (see Henry and Koski (2010) for the discussion of this rule) with the intention to curb this price manipulation. One loophole of these rules are that investors can short sell the stocks using options, rather than directly shorting selling the stocks (Danielsen and Sorescu, 2001).

Masulis and Kim (2010) show that there are positive order imbalance before the SEO and negative order imbalance afterwards, and order imbalance is positively related to the degree of underpricing. They attribute these patterns to the market maker's inventory management and underwriter's price support activities.

The American SEC's adoption of Rule 10b-21 invokes some disputes, which include Safieddine and Jr. Wilhelm (1996), Chemmanur et al. (2009), and Chemmanur and Jiao (2011). The papers on Rule 10b-21 provides evidence, although indirect, on the short-selling prior to the SEO (see the subsection on this topic). Rule 10b-21 was adopted on August 25, 1988. In April 1997, Rule 10b-21 was replaced by Rule 105. Corwin (2003) also includes the Rule 10b-21 as an explanatory variable in determining the SEO discount, and shows that the SEO discounts increase after the adoption of Rule 10b-21. Henry and Koski (2010) discuss Rule 105.

Gibson et al. (2004) show that institutional investors are able to identify outperforming SEOs. Field and Lowry (2009) posit an interesting question. They argue that institutional investors achieve higher return on IPOs simply because they use the readily public available information more efficiently than individual investors do.

7.5 Market reaction and long term performance

A lot of empirical evidence shows that the stock price runs up one year before the issue, the market negatively reacts to the announcement (Lease et al., 1991), and the stock underperforms the reasonable benchmark in the long run. The negative reaction and the long term underperformance are confusing. Several explanations have been proposed, which can be categorized into two lines: rational and irrational explanation.

Explanations for negatively positive reactions to and long-term underperformance after SEO include:

1. Market timing. SEO firm managements take advantage of the "window of opportunities" when their stocks are over-valued (see Loughran and Ritter, 1997).
2. Investor over-optimism at the announcement, which results in long term underperformance after SEO (Daniel et al., 1998). As for the nature of the investor over-optimism, Loughran and Ritter (1997) and Hertzel et al. (2002) suggest that both management and investors are over-optimistic about the capital investment (thus, over-confidence over the capital expenditures)

and the growth opportunities.

3. Investor under-reaction to the information conveyed by the announcement, which results in the same direction drift.

Prevailing explanation for the market's negative reaction to public SEOs is that they convey unfavorable information. Miller and Rock (1985) show the market interprets unexpected SEO as bad news. Pecking order theory (Myers and Majluf, 1984) also supports this explanation in that managers shouldn't resort to external equities before the internal funds are exhausted.

For similar logic, the market positively reacts to private placements because they convey favorable information: "the willingness of private placement investors to commit funds to a firm, together with management's decision to forego public issues, conveys to the market management's belief that the firm is undervalued" (Hertzel and Smith, 1993, p. 460).

Barberis and Huang (2008) is an obvious exception in the irrational explanations. They apply prospect theory to asset pricing, and find that contrary to the traditional expected utility theory, investors will value the positively skewed stock more highly than that suggested by the "rational" expected utility theory, thus such kind of stocks on average exhibit long term lower return. If, as they conjectured, the SEO stocks are positively skewed, then there is no wonder to see lower average long term returns. See also Anderson and Garcia-Feijóo (2006), Lamont (2000), Polk and Sapienza (2002), and Titman et al. (2004), who attribute the underperformance to overinvestment.

Gibson et al. (2004) show that SEOs with increased institutional ownership outperform the benchmarks, indicating that institutional investors are able to identify outperforming SEOs. Akhigbe et al. (2006) document the "surprise" that issue type plays a role in determining the market response and the long term performance.

Benninga et al. (2005) provide an interesting explanation for the long run underperformance of IPO firms, by taking into account the option value of reprivatization (Carlson et al., 2006, p. 1011). They argue that "a decline in returns following investment is a natural consequence of growth option exercise." Manove (1989) relates the insider trading with the short-term market reactions to the firm's announcement of issuing new equity to finance an investment.

Lease et al. (1991) argue that the offering day negative return documented in event studies is artificial, because it is due to the selling pressure (buy-sell imbalance) on the offering day. They also argue that the immediate days following the offering day have negative, rather than positive, returns, if using the midpoint of the closing transactions rather than the closing price to estimate the returns. They attribute this phenomenon to the specialist's and underwriter's effort to lower their inventory.

Lease et al. (1991) point out the inaccuracy of SEO event dates in the SDC database. We should therefore use McLaughlin et al.'s (1996) method to determine the SEO event dates.

Chapter 8
Behavioral explanation

8.1 General discussion on the behavioral explanation

The past three decades have witnessed great developments of behavioral finance and behavioral economics. In this chapter, we will go through some behavioral explanations to the market dynamics and investor behaviors. Before we dive deep into these issues, one should keep in mind that behavioral explanations do not necessarily mean that investors are irrational. The difference between rational expectations and behavioral explanations have become smaller like they used to be when behavioral explanations first appeared on top tier finance and economics journals.

Shefrin (2005) summarizes the behavioral asset pricing literature. Vissing-Jorgensen (2003, p. 190) argues that "information and/or transaction costs represent a possible rational explanation of behaviors that involve too little action or too simple actions relative to the theoretical benchmark. I argued that many such behaviors tend to diminish with investor wealth and sophistication and thus that information and transaction costs should be seriously considered as an explanation. As an example, a simple calculation showed that, given the observed distribution of financial wealth, an annual cost of about \$55 is enough to explain the choices of half of these who do not invest in the stock market." Also see Section 2 of Vissing-Jorgensen (2003, pp. 141–144) for a discussion of the vagueness of current empirical evidence to distinguish rational and behavioral explanations.

Daniel and Titman (1999) first argue for the notion of "adaptive efficiency." Besides this notion, there is also so-called Quasi-Bayesian: "decision markets, because of one or more of the documented cognitive biases, have a mistaken view of the world or inappropriately with its various dimensions, but otherwise act as Bayesians in updating beliefs. An important property of this class of models is that rational decision making obtains in the limit as the parameters representing the cognitive biases approach zero, or as the biases disappear" (Asparouhova et al., 2009, p. 1766)."

Brav and Heaton (2002, p. 575) summarize the two key assumptions of the traditional rational models: "[Traditional] theory has two characteristic features. First, investors are assumed to have essentially complete knowledge of the fundamental structure of their economy. Second, investors are assumed to be completely rational information processors who make optimal statistical decisions. Put another way, investors in the benchmark theory have 'access both to the correct specification of the 'true' economic model and to unbiased estimators of its coefficients'" (Friedman, 1979, p. 38). Brav and Heaton (2002) label the behavioral models as those which relax the second assumption. Notably, Brav and Heaton (2002, p. 576) mention another strand of models which "maintains the complete rationality assumption, but relaxes the assumption that investors have complete knowledge of the fundamental structure of the economy." The authors call these models "rational structural uncertainty" models.

Behavioral consistency theory presumes that individuals behave consistently across situations. Studies include: positive relations between all the risky behaviors (Barsky et al., 1997); CEOs' overconfidence in their personal loans and the corporate investment decisions (Malmendier and Tate, 2005); fund managers' donations and their choice on socially responsible investments (Hong and Kostovetsky, 2012); CEOs' personal leverage and corporate leverage (Cronqvist et al., 2012).

8.2 Disposition effect and prospect theory

Disposition effect was first proposed by Shefrin and Statman (1985). Disposition effect refers to the behavior that investors hold onto losing investment, and sell profitable investment. Notice that disposition effect could be a manifestation of contrarian strategy.

Grinblatt and Keloharju (2001b) show evidence that all investor categories exhibit disposition effect. And this effect is attenuated in December due to the tax-loss selling. Many attribute the disposition effect to the prospect theory proposed by Kahneman and Tversky (1979). The prospect theory argues that "value of [utility] is assigned to gains and losses rather than final assets ... The value function is normally concave for gains, commonly convex for losses, and is generally steeper for losses than for gains" (p. 263). See Baker et al. (2012, p. 52) for the papers that apply the reference points story. One often employed reference point is the stock's 52-week high.

House money effect was first documented by Thaler and Johnson (1990). Loss aversion and house money effect have different prediction in the relation between profit and risk taking. See Coval and Shumway (2005, p. 3, 5 7) for the discussion. Coval and Shumway (2005) show that investors tend to take fewer risks when they experience profit in the morning. The authors further show that when the losses are widespread, volatility is larger.

8.3 Overconfidence and over-reaction

Odean (1998b) propose a model in which investors overestimate the precision of their knowledge, and thus trade excessively. The idea is that since overconfident investors believe more strongly in their own valuations on the stocks, it intensifies the differences of opinions among investors. So in Odean's view, excessive trading is the symptom of overconfidence. Lundeberg et al. (1994) find that men are more confident than women. Barber and Odean (2001) show empirical evidence that men trade more than women, and because excessive trading hurts investment performance, men earn lower return than do women.

Empirical evidence has shown that stock prices under-react to news over horizons of 1–12 months, and over-react to news over long horizons of 3–5 years.

If investors under-react in the short run and over-react in the long run, the stock prices will exhibit the momentum effect in the short run and the contrarian effect in the long run. Put differently, stock returns are positively autocorrelated in the short run, and negatively autocorrelated in the long run. So this literature is closely related to the momentum and contrarian literature. This literature is also related to the positive feedback trading literature which discusses the relation between investors trading and stock returns.

Notice the following summary from Barberis et al. (1998, p. 312): "Bernard and Thomas (1990) find that [company earnings] series exhibit an autocorrelation of about 0.34 at a lag of one quarter, 0.19 at two quarters, 0.06 at three quarters, and −0.24 at four quarters. That is, earnings changes exhibit a slight trend at one-, two-, and three-quarter horizons and a slight reversal after a year. In interpreting the evidence, Bernard conjectures that market participants do not recognize the positive autocorrelations in earnings changes, and in fact believe that earnings follow a random walk. This belief causes them to underreact to earnings announcements."

Fama and French (1996) argue that their multifactor model can account for the overreaction in the long run. But their pricing model cannot account for the underreaction in the short run. Behavioral explanations can be found in De Long et al. (1990a, b), Cutler et al. (1991), Barberis et al. (1998), Daniel et al. (1998), Rabin (2002), and Rabin and Vayanos (2010).

Barberis et al. (1998) propose a model which relies on two behaviorial biases: representativeness and conservatism. In particular, "[the investor] believes that the behavior of a given firm's earnings moves between two 'states' or 'regimes'. In the first state, earnings are mean-reverting. In the second state, they trend, i.e., are likely to rise further after an increase... Each period, the investor observes earnings, and uses this information to update his beliefs about which state he is in... Specifically, when a positive earnings surprise is followed by another positive surprise, the investor raises the likelihood that he is in the trending regime, whereas when a positive surprise is followed by a negative surprise, the investor raises the likelihood that he is in the mean-reverting regime."

Rabin (2002) and Rabin and Vayanos (2010) rely on the law of small numbers, which we will discuss in a separate subsection. In comparing their model and Barberis et al.'s (1998), Rabin and Vayanos (2010, p. 734) comment: "BSV provide a psychological foundation for their assumptions by appealing to a combination of biases: the conservatism bias for the reversal regime and the representativeness bias for the streak regime. Our model, by contrast, not only derives such biases from the single underlying bias of the gambler's fallacy, but in doing so provides predictions as to which biases are likely to appear in different informational settings."

8.4 Awareness, familiarity, and attention

Home bias was found by French and Poterba (1991), Cooper and Kaplanis

(1994), and Tesar and Werner (1995). Home bias can be due to restrictions on international investment (Stulz, 1981a,b), for example the regulations on foreign currency. Grinblatt and Keloharju (2001a, pp. 1053–1054) argue that "home bias may be part of a larger phenomenon in which investors exhibit a preference for familiar companies. Familiarity has many facets. The firm's language, culture, and distance from the investor are three important familiarity attributes that might explain an investor's preference for certain firms." Grinblatt and Keloharju (2001a) find these three attributes affect the investor's choice. Moreover, more sophisticated investors are less likely to be affected by these attributes.

Conventional asset pricing literature assumes that investors are able to analyze all the securities in the market, a task that is hard even for the most up-to-date super computers today. Naturally, behavioral finance assumes that investors have only limited capacity to analyze the investment alternatives, or have only limited attentions.

Notice that there are rational models that can be consistent with the empirical evidence provided by the behavioral finance literature. For example, Hirshleifer et al. (1994) provide a model in which some investors obtain information earlier than others. Therefore, the sequential information prompts investors to behave like herding. Moreover, the earlier informed investors' expected utility increases with the number of later informed investors. There are multi equilibria and investors may also herd on certain stocks, while ignoring other stocks.

8.5 Law of small numbers

Tversky and Kahneman (1971) coin the term of "the law of small numbers." The law of small numbers refers to people's erroneous intuitions about the laws of chance. In particular, "people view a sample of randomly drawn from a population as highly representative, that is, similar to the population in all essential characteristics. Consequently, they expect any two samples drawn from a particular population to be more similar to one another and to the population than sampling theory predicts, at least for small samples" (p. 105). So "subjects act as if every segment of the random sequence must reflect the true proportion: if the sequence has strayed from the population proportion, a corrective bias in the other direction is expected. This has been called the gambler's fallacy" (p. 106). Furthermore, this bias leads people to underestimate the variability of the small sample, thus they "will have exaggerated confidence in the validity of conclusions based on small samples" (p. 106). As Tversky and Kahneman's (1971) experiment was conducted on a handful of attendees of the meetings of the Mathematical Psychology Group and of the American Psychological Association, their evidence shows that this bias is "shared by naive subjects and by trained scientists."

Asparouhova et al. (2009) conduct an experiment to compare the behavioral biases in Rabin's (2002) model and in Barberis et al.'s (1998) model. The differences in the behavioral biases are the following. Barberis et al. (1998) rely on two biases: conservatism and representativeness. And agents are assumed to believe that the process switches between a reversal regime and a continuation regime. This assumption implies that the investors monotonically estimate a higher probability of being in a continuation regime when streak length increases. Rabin (2002) relies on one bias: the law of small numbers, which leads to two biased beliefs depending on the process facing investors. These two biased beliefs are gambler's fallacy and hot-hand fallacy. In particular, a short streak generates gambler's fallacy and a long streak generates hot-hand fallacy. Therefore, agents initially expect a reversal when facing a short streak, and then switch to the expectation of continuation when the streak length increases. In Asparouhova et al.'s (2009) model, "subjects are presented with randomly generated sequences of eight binary (UP or DOWN) outcomes and then asked to make a probability assessment on the likelihood that the next (ninth) outcome will be UP" (p. 1767). The experiment shows that "when streak length is short (less than or equal to 3), subjects are more likely to expect a reversal the longer the streak... The above effect reverses for longer streaks; i.e., conditional on streak length exceeding 3, subjects are more likely to expect that the streak will continue the longer the streak... [That is,] the effect of gambler's fallacy strengthens initially as the streak length increases and weakens as the streak becomes longer" (p. 1768).

8.6 Rational structural uncertainty models

Rational structural uncertainty models have two features. First, agents are rational in that they consistently make the optimal statistical decisions. Second, they do not have complete knowledge on the structure of the underlying economy (Brav and Heaton, 2002). In this sense, these models are not irrational behavioral explanations. Irrational behavioral explanations resort to irrational decision making, while maintain that agents have complete knowledge on the economy structure.

Brav and Heaton (2002) compare the rational structural uncertainty model and irrational models. The authors argue that these two strands of models are observationally indistinguishable, at least when explaining over- and underreactions. They show that "the representativeness heuristic involves heavy weighting of recent data, while conservatism leads to underweighting of recent data. In the structural uncertainty model, beliefs about the stability of valuation-relevant parameters determine the respective importance in estimates of those parameters of older data, newer data, and an investor's prior beliefs... [The structural uncertainty] estimator involves heavy weighting of recent data (and excessive certainty) when applied in a stable environment, just as with the [representativeness heuristic] estimator. This is the situation when the [structural uncertainty] estimator exhibits overreaction... The [structural uncertainty] estimator underweights new data immediately after a change, since old (and, by definition, irrelevant) data enter the estimate, just as the [behavioral conservatism] estimator. This is the situation when the [structural uncertainty] estimator exhibits underreaction (drift)... Investors placing low weight on new data may be acting irrationally and displaying conservatism, but they also may be placing more weight on old data and prior beliefs in the (rational) belief that the underlying parameters might not have changed. Alternatively, investors placing heavy weight on recent data may be acting irrationally and displaying the representativeness heuristic, but they also may be placing more weight on recent data in the (rational) belief that the underlying parameters are unstable, rendering the older data less relevant to their estimates" (pp. 590–591). The authors also show that "the overconfidence effect will occur simultaneously with the heavy weighting of recent data" (p. 591).

Chapter 9
Modeling economic behavior

A game is an interaction among players. There are two aspects characterizing a game: sequence of moves and information set. The sequence of moves classifies games into simultaneous versus sequential games, or static versus dynamic games. Information set classifies games into perfect information and imperfect information games. In this chapter we first discuss the simplest game, in which players move simultaneously and all of them are perfectly informed. Then we proceed to discuss sequential games, while assuming perfect information. After that, we discuss games in which players move simultaneously, while some or all of them are imperfectly informed. Lastly, we combine the characteristics of sequentiality and imperfect information.

9.1 Nash equilibrium

9.1.1 Dominant and dominated strategy

If regardless of what the opponents play, a strategy yields strictly higher payoff than any other strategies, then this strategy is strictly dominant. Formally, a strategy $s_i \in S_i$ is a strictly dominant strategy for player *i*, if for all $s'_i \neq s_i$, we have $u_i(s_i, s_{-i}) > u_i(s'_i, s_{-i})$. A strategy $s_i \in S_i$ is strictly dominated for player i if there exists a strategy $s'_i \neq s_i$ such that for all $s_{-i} \in S_{-i}$, we have $u_i(s'_i, s_{-i}) > u_i(s_i, s_{-i})$. In this case we call strategy s'_i strictly dominates s_i .

Similarly, we can define weakly dominated strategy by changing the above inequality to $u_i(s'_i, s_{-i}) \geq u_i(s_i, s_{-i})$. So compared to strictly dominated strategy, a weakly dominated strategy yields the same payoff when the opponents play some actions. Do not confuse weakly dominated strategy with no dominance. If a strategy yields higher payoff when opponents play some actions, and yields lower payoff when opponents plays other actions, then this strategy is neither dominant nor (weakly or strictly) dominated.

In most cases, we only say a pure strategy is strictly dominated, we seldom say a mixed strategy is strictly dominated. It makes sense because if a pure strategy is strictly dominated, it should be eliminated even if mixed strategy is allowed. That is, a mixed strategy that includes a strictly dominated pure strategy is surely dominated.

When mixed strategy is allowed, to test whether a pure strategy is strictly dominated, we do not need to concern about the mixed strategy of opponents at all. For the reason of this point, see Proposition 8.B.1 of Mas-Colell et al. (1995, p. 241). However, we need to consider the mixed strategy of the player under consideration. That is, when mixed strategy is allowed, to test whether a pure strategy s_i of a specific player is strictly dominated, we need to find a mixed or pure strategy of this player that yields strictly higher payoff than does s_i regardless of what pure strategies the opponents play.

By and large, weakly dominated strategy helps little when we are trying to find the equilibrium. However, it does help somewhat when we are dealing with sequential games. The common feature of dominant and dominated strategy is that both of them consider the comparison regardless of how opponents act. Strictly dominated strategy requires that at least one strategy yields a strictly higher payoff.

A rationalizable strategy is such a strategy responding to some of the opponents' strategy. A similar notion as the strictly dominated strategy emerges in the context of rationality, the *never-best response*. In a game in which mixed strategy is not allowed, the set of the never-best responses is larger than the set of strictly dominated strategies. So elimination of never-best response strategies helps us narrow down the candidates for pure strategy Nash equilibrium. This property does not hold when mixed strategy is allowed. In fact, when mixed strategy is allowed, the set of the strictly dominated strategies and the set of never-best responses are the same. That is, never-best response is equivalent to strictly dominated strategy. So unsurprisingly, a never-best response when mixed strategy is not allowed might be a best response when mixed strategies are allowed. See the example of Figure 139.2 in Osborne (2004, p. 139). Also notice that all the above discussion on rationality holds only when the players have only finite actions to choose.

Rationality implies that the strategy is a best response to some belief on the opponents' strategies. Then Nash equilibrium adds an additional requirement to rationality, i.e. the belief is also correct.

9.1.2 Definition of Nash equilibrium

A Nash equilibrium is a mutual best response strategy. So a simple way to find pure strategy Nash equilibrium in a strategic game, if it exists, is to underline each player's best response to each opponent's action. If a cell has both actions underlined, then this cell is a pure strategy Nash equilibrium.

Iterated elimination of strictly dominated strategy may lead to a pure strategy Nash equilibrium, and any elimination order gives the same result. This order irrelevance property does not hold for weakly dominated strategy. In fact, a weakly dominated strategy might be a pure strategy Nash equilibrium. See Osborne (2004, Figure 47.2 on p. 47) for an example.

Strictly dominated strategies appear in neither a pure strategy Nash equilibrium nor a mixed one. In other words, if a pure strategy is strictly dominated, then it should be deleted from the payoff matrix, regardless whether mixed strategy is allowed.

A mixed strategy Nash equilibrium must have the following property. Given the opponents' pure strategies included in his Nash equilibrium mixed strategy. Notice that the explanation for this point is incomplete in Osborne (2004, p. 116). The properties follows because if among the actions included in player 's mixed strategy, one yields higher payoff than do all the others, then he may choose this one and assigns zero probability to all the others. This contradicts with the presumption that the equilibrium mixed strategy assigns positive probability to all the pure strategies included in the mixed strategy. Since the expected payoffs to every pure strategy included in the equilibrium mixed strategy are all equal, this property also implies that any of the pure strategies in the mixed strategy and any of other mixed strategies that include the same pure strategies as does the equilibrium mixed strategy have the same expected payoff, and all of them are the best responses to the opponents' strategy specified by the equilibrium mixed strategy.

A mixed strategy consists of several actions for each player, and the player assigns positive probabilities to these actions. Suppose $\alpha*$ is a mixed strategy equilibrium, and $\{a_i\}$ is the set of actions that player i assigns positive probabilities, then each action in $\{a_i\}$ is a best response to the mixed strategy equilibrium α^*, actually each action in $\{a_i\}$ generates the same payoff to player i given that his opponent plays the mixed strategy α^* ; and furthermore any mixed strategy consisting of and only of $\{a_i\}$ is also a best response to the equilibrium.

To find all mixed strategy Nash equilibriums, first iteratively delete all the strictly dominated strategies. And then check all the combinations of the pure strategies to see if for each player the following two conditions are held: (1) the expected payoff to every action included in the mixed strategy are all equal, call this expected payoff E; (2) the expected payoff to every action not included in the mixed strategy is not higher than E. The combinations of the pure strategies should include the cases in which one player plays pure strategy and the others play mixed strategies. See Osborne (2004, Example 139.2 on p. 139) for an example.

The central idea of Nash equilibrium is that players have no incentive to deviate from the equilibrium strategy. "No incentive" is a weak condition. A deviating player may be either worse off or indifferent. If the deviation makes the player worse off, we say this equilibrium is a **strict Nash equilibrium**. Notice that only pure strategy equilibrium can be candidates of strict equilibrium. Any action in a mixed strategy equilibrium and any mixed strategy consists of the same actions, but different probabilities, like the equilibrium strategy, generate the same payoffs. That is, mixed strategy equilibrium is necessarily non-strict.

9.1.3 Evolutionary stability

In a symmetric two-player game, the equilibrium α^* is **evolutionarily stable** if for every strategy β that is the best response of opponents' strategy specified by α^*, $U(\beta,\beta) < U(\alpha^*,\beta)$ always holds. The idea is that the mutants must choose best responses to the equilibrium. $U(\beta,\beta) < U(\alpha^*,\beta)$ indicates that when facing a mutant, a *regular* does better than does a mutant. Therefore, the mutants will die out.

The above definition also specifies how to test the evolutionary stability. First, notice that only equilibrium can be tested. Second, given that one player plays equilibrium strategy, find the best response to this strategy. Third, test whether the inequality above holds. Specifically, if the equilibrium is strict, it is necessarily evolutionary stable. But strict equilibrium only exists when mixed strategy is not allowed. So when mixed strategy is allowed, the concept of strict equilibrium helps little in testing the evolutionary stability.

For the mixed strategy equilibrium, the trick to find the best response is to construct a mixed strategy that consists of the same actions as does the equilibrium. To establish the mixed strategy equilibrium being evolutionarily stable, just show that there's no probability schemes over the actions, except that specified by the equilibrium strategy, such that yields a higher payoff than the equilibrium strategy when facing this mutant strategy.

For the mixed strategy equilibrium, the trick to find the best response is to construct a mixed strategy that consists of the same actions as does the equilibrium. To establish the mixed strategy equilibrium being evolutionarily stable, show that there's no probability schemes over the actions, except that specified by the equilibrium strategy, such that yields a higher payoff than the equilibrium strategy when facing this mutant strategy.

Osborne (2004, p. 401) states: "A pure strategy may be immune to invasion by mutants that follow any pure strategy but may not be immune to invasion by mutants that follow some mixed strategy. Stated briefly, though a pure strategy Nash equilibrium is a mixed strategy Nash equilibrium, an action that is evolutionarily stable [when mixed strategy is not allowed] is not necessarily an evolutionarily stable strategy [when mixed strategy is allowed]." But, a strict pure strategy equilibrium is evolutionarily stable no matter mixed strategy is allowed or not, because there is no best response to the equilibrium except the equilibrium strategy itself.

9.1.4 Continuous strategy space

Cournot (choosing quantity) and Bertrand (choosing price) are two examples of continuous strategy games. A typical Cournot game assumes two firms have respective cost c_1, c_2, the market price is determined by $a - Q_1 - Q_2$. We can show that the equilibrium quantity is $Q_i^* = \frac{1}{3}(a + c_{-i} - 2c_i)$, the equilibrium profit is $\frac{1}{9}(a + c_{-i} - 2c_i)^2$, and the equilibrium price is $\frac{1}{3}(a + c_i + c_{-i})$.

Let us consider a special case of two-player game. Suppose in such a game, each player can choose an action xi from a continuous strategy space. Further suppose the payoff functions are the same for both players. Then we can show that

$$\frac{\partial u(x_i, x_{-i})}{\partial x_i} = 0$$

Since x_i is a function of x_{-i}, so taking derivate with respect to x_{-i} yields

$$\frac{\partial^2 u(x_i, x_{-i})}{\partial x_i \partial x_{-i}} + \frac{\partial^2 u(x_i, x_{-i})}{\partial x_i^2} \frac{\mathrm{d}x_i}{\mathrm{d}x_{-i}} = 0$$

Simplifying this equation we get

$$\frac{\mathrm{d}x_i}{\mathrm{d}x_{-i}} = \frac{\partial^2 u(x_i, x_{-i})}{\partial x_i \partial x_{-i}} / \left(- \frac{\partial^2 u(x_i, x_{-i})}{\partial x_i^2} \right)$$

We typically assume $\frac{\partial^2 u(x_i, x_{-i})}{\partial x_i^2} < 0$, because otherwise we can't find an optimal x_i that maximizes $u(x_i, x_{-i})$. So the sign of $\frac{\mathrm{d}x_i}{\mathrm{d}x_{-i}}$ is determined by the sign of $\frac{\partial^2 u(x_i, x_{-i})}{\partial x_i \partial x_{-i}}$. If $\frac{\partial^2 u(x_i, x_{-i})}{\partial x_i \partial x_{-i}} > 0$, then $\frac{\mathrm{d}x_i}{\mathrm{d}x_{-i}} > 0$ meaning the optimal action of both players move to the same direction, i.e., when one player *increases* his optimal action, the other player will also do so. In this case, the two actions are known as **strategic complements**, and the game is called **supermodular**. Otherwise, when $\frac{\partial^2 u(x_i, x_{-i})}{\partial x_i \partial x_{-i}} < 0$, $\frac{\mathrm{d}x_i}{\mathrm{d}x_{-i}} < 0$ meaning if one player *increases* his action, the other player will optimally do the opposite. The two actions are known as **strategic substitutes**, and the game is called **submodular**.

9.2 Bayesian games

The first additional characteristic relative to the simplest static and perfect information game is *states*. Let S_i denote the state space for player i, then the *state space of the game* is given by $S = \prod_i S_i$. So suppose player *i* has s_i states, then S should have $S = \sum_i s_i$ elements. For example, a firm's, say firm 1's, production cost may be high or low, which defines two states, denoted as $\mathcal{S}_1 = \{H, L\}$. In addition, the other firm, say firm 2, may or may not whether its opponent's cost is high or low, which defines two states, denoted as $\mathcal{S}_2 = \{K, N\}$. So these two assumptions define four states in total. Let us denote the state space of the game as $\mathcal{S} = \mathcal{S}_1 \times \mathcal{S}_2 = \{HK, LK, HN, LN\}$. So these two assumptions define four states in total. Let us denote the *state space of the game* as $S = S_1 \times S_2 = \{HK, LK, HN, LN\}$. Notice **the state space of the game should be identical for all players.**

The second additional characteristics is *information* set for each player. Let us denote player *i*'s information set by Ω_1 , and n_i as the number of elements in Ω_1 . In the above example, if we assume that firm 1 does not know whether firm 2 knows firm 1's cost, and firm 2 may or may not know firm 1's cost, then the information set for the two firms are $\Omega_1 = \{\{LK\} \cup \{LN\}, \{HK\} \cup \{HN\}\}$, $\Omega_2 = \{\{LN\} \cup \{KN\}, LK, HK\}$. Notice that **the information set must be the subsets of state space.** Sometimes, we say that the elements of the information set defines *the types of the player*.

To make the problem tractable, we have to help agents form prior beliefs. Specifically, player *i* in each type (i.e. elements of his information set Ω_1) must attach probabilities to every element of player 's information set (probabilities of every type of player). Here we assume that every player's information sets are common knowledge among all players. So player *i*'s prior belief on player *i* can be represented by a $n_i \times n_{-i}$ matrix, where n_j denotes the number of types player *i* could be, i.e. the number of elements in player *j*'s information set. In the above example, the prior beliefs of the two firms are

$$\mathbf{B}_1 = \begin{pmatrix} 1-\pi & \pi & 0 \\ 1-\pi & 0 & \pi \end{pmatrix} \qquad \mathbf{B}_2 = \begin{pmatrix} \theta & 1-\theta \\ 1 & 0 \\ 0 & 1 \end{pmatrix}$$

We can interpret these two belief matrices as follows. When firm 1 is of low cost, he believes that firm 2 knows firm 1 is so with probability π , and firm 2 knows nothing with probability 1-π .[1] Similar interpretation applies to the second row of $\mathbf{B}_1$. For $\mathbf{B}_2$, the first row shows that when firm 2 does not know firm 1's

1 Obviously in this case firm 1 attaches zero probability to the event that firm 2 believes firm 1 is of high cost

cost, firm 2 believes that firm 2 is of low cost with probability , and of high cost with probability $1-\theta$. The second (third) row shows that when firm 2 knows that firm 1 is of low (high) cost, it assigns probability 1 to this event.

Next we define the actions for when each **player *i* chooses an action for every type he could be**. That is, if there are n_i elements in player *i*'s information set, his strategy is defined by a vector of order n_i , denoted as $\mathbf{a}_i$. Let $a_{i,j}$ be the *j*th element of vector $\mathbf{a}_i$. That is, $a_{i,j}$ represents player *i*'s action when he is of *j*th type.

Then, let us consider the payoffs. Suppose when player *i* is in his *j*th type, and his opponent —*i* is in his *k* th type, then the payoff to player *i* is $f_{i,j}(a_{i,j}, a_{-i,k})$. Notice the function *f* has only two subscripts: *i* and *j* . This is because in equilibrium, player *i* chooses one action when he is in the *j*th type, regardless of what his opponents play. Also define $g_{i,j}(a_{-i,k})$ as

$$\frac{\partial}{\partial a_{i,j}} f_{i,j}(a_{i,j}, a_{-i,k})$$

Notice that $g_{i,j}(a_{-i,k})$ indicates it is a function of $a_{-i,k}$ as long as $a_{i,j}$ is given. Further define matrix $\mathbf{G}_j$, whose *m*th×*n*th element is $g_{i,m}(a_{-i,n})$. Then calculate diag $(\mathbf{B}_i\mathbf{G}'_i)\mathbf{1}_{n_i\times 1} = \mathbf{0}$[2], which yields n_i equations. Repeat this procedure for every player *i*, and collect all the equations, we have a system of $\sum_i n_i$ equations with $\sum_i n_i$ unknowns.

In the above example, each firm chooses its output level $q_{i,j}$ as its action, i.e. $a_{i,j}$. If we further define the market price as $\alpha - q_1 - q_2$, then it's easily seen that $g_{i,j}(q_{-i,k}) = \alpha - q_{-i,k} - c_{i,j} - 2q_{i,j}$. Specially,

$$\mathbf{G}_1 = \begin{pmatrix} \alpha - q_{2,1} - c_L - 2q_{1,1} & \alpha - q_{2,2} - c_L - 2q_{1,1} & \alpha - q_{2,3} - c_L - 2q_{1,1} \\ \alpha - q_{2,1} - c_H - 2q_{1,2} & \alpha - q_{2,2} - c_H - 2q_{1,2} & \alpha - q_{2,3} - c_H - 2q_{1,2} \end{pmatrix}$$

$$\mathbf{G}_2 = \begin{pmatrix} \alpha - q_{1,1} - c_2 - 2q_{2,1} & \alpha - q_{1,2} - c_2 - 2q_{2,1} \\ \alpha - q_{1,1} - c_2 - 2q_{2,2} & \alpha - q_{1,2} - c_2 - 2q_{2,2} \\ \alpha - q_{1,1} - c_2 - 2q_{2,3} & \alpha - q_{1,2} - c_2 - 2q_{2,3} \end{pmatrix}$$

---

2 $\mathbf{1}_{n_i\times 1}$ is a vector of n_i , whose elements are all 1. This strange expression represents this calculation. Both $\mathbf{B}_i$ and $\mathbf{G}_i$ are $n_i \times n_{-i}$ matrices, then we have multiple elements in the same position, and then sum the elements of every row, thus we obtain a vector of order n_i .

9.3 Utility maximization models

Let the utility function be $U(w) =- \mathrm{e}^{-\gamma w}$. The initial wealth is w_0, among which α_0 is on risky asset, and $1-\alpha_0$ is on risk free asset. The terminal payment of each unit risky asset is $\widetilde{R} \sim N(\mu, \sigma^2)$, and the terminal payment of each unit risk free asset is R_f. The investor needs to rebalance her portfolio to maximize the terminal utility. Suppose she decides α of her initial wealth should go to the risky asset. So the terminal wealth is $w = \alpha w_0 R + (1-\alpha) w_0 R_f$, and the expected terminal utility is

$$\begin{aligned} \mathbb{E}\big(U(w)\big) &= \int_{-\infty}^{\infty} - \mathrm{e}^{-\gamma[\alpha w_0 R+(1-\alpha) w_0 R_f]} \frac{1}{\sigma\sqrt{2\pi}} \mathrm{e}^{-\frac{(R-\mu)^2}{2\sigma^2}} \mathrm{d}R \\ &= -\mathrm{e}^{\gamma w_0 \left(\frac{\gamma w_0 \sigma^2}{2}\alpha^2+(R_f-\mu)\alpha-R_f\right)} \end{aligned}$$

Maximizing $\mathbb{E}\big(U(w)\big)$ with respect to α amounts to maximizing $\frac{\gamma w_0 \sigma^2}{2}\alpha^2 + (R_f-\mu)\alpha - R_f$, and we have $\alpha^* = \frac{\mu - R_f}{\gamma w_0 \sigma^2}$. This result shows that the optimal position on the risky asset is $w_0\alpha^* = \frac{\mu - R_f}{\gamma\sigma^2}$, which is independent from the initial position and the total wealth, and is dependent only on the belief on the return distribution and the investor's risk aversion.

Chapter 10
Mathematical techniques for economic modeling

We use mathematical models to depict the real world, or more precisely, to depict how the real world behaves. The real world's behavior concerns two questions: I) what is the *equilibrium*, and II) how does the real world evolves. In my point of view, the latter is more fundamental in that equilibrium can be viewed as the *steady state* of the long term evolution. Most researches, however, do not explicitly distinguish between these two aspects. Rather, they often focus on the equilibrium outcome, avoiding to answer on how the equilibrium is achieved.

To model the evolution or dynamics of the real world, we usually use *difference* or *differential* equations. Difference equations deal with discrete time models and differential equations deal with *continuous time* models. The idea of using difference or differential equations is as follows. Common sense or intuition or academic researches show how the object of interest evolves at an arbitrary instant of time. This gives us a difference or differential equation to describe the object. Then we can solve this equation, and furthermore understand what the steady state is, if it exists. As I mentioned before, this steady state is exactly the equilibrium. So we begin this part by first discussing how to solve difference and differential equations. We also discuss the existence of the steady state. In discrete time models, *fixed point theorem* concerns the existence of steady state.

Another idea of modeling the real world is to depict how economic agents make optimal decisions. To answer this question, we resort to optimization theory.

Both of the above two modeling approaches leave no room for *probabilistic events*. Everything in the model is *deterministic*. That is, given the beginning state of the world, we know for sure what state the world lies in at any particular time. Although appearing unrealistic, this deterministic way simplifies our modeling task.

10.1 Difference equations

A simplest linear difference equation may be written as $x_{t+1} = ax_t$. It's easily seen that this equation can be rewritten as $x_t = a^t x_0$.

If the difference equation is $\mathbf{x}_{t+1} = \mathbf{A}\mathbf{x}_t$, then when **A** is a diagonal matrix, the system is decoupled, which means the i th element of $\mathbf{x}_{t+1}$ depends on the ith element of $\mathbf{x}_t$ only. If **A** is not diagonal but is diagonalizable, then we can rewrite the difference equation as $\mathbf{x}_{t+1} = \mathbf{P}^{-1}\mathbf{D}\mathbf{P}\mathbf{x}_t$. Let $\mathbf{u}_t = \mathbf{P}\mathbf{x}_t$, then $\mathbf{P}\mathbf{u}_{t+1} = \mathbf{D}\mathbf{u}_t$. Since **D** is a diagonal matrix with elements of the eigenvalues of **A**, $\mathbf{P}\mathbf{u}_t = \mathbf{D}^t\mathbf{u}_0$. Converting **u** back to **x** , we get $\mathbf{x}_t = \mathbf{P}^{-1}\mathbf{D}^t\mathbf{P}\mathbf{x}_0$.

10.2 Differential equations

Only a small portion of the differential equations have analytical solutions.

10.2.1 Existence and uniqueness of the solutions

A first order differential equation can be written as $\frac{dx}{dt} = \mathbf{F}(t, \mathbf{x})$, where **x** denotes a vector. If **F** and **F'** are both continuous, then a unique solution exists at least locally. That is, if we know the initial condition, then at least around this initial $\mathbf{x}(t = t_0)$, there is one and only one path for the variable vector **x** to evolve. And actually if some conditions are met, the unique path (solution) exists over the whole interval $t \in (-\infty, \infty)$, or $t \in (t_0, \infty)$.

In summary, given the differential equation(s) and initial/terminal condition, we can safely assume that there exists a unique path defined by the differential equation(s), regardless of whether or not we can find the analytical solution to the differential equation(s). This property also indicates that given the differential equation(s) and the initial condition, we are very likely to arrive at a "determined" terminal condition.

10.2.2 Solving one-variable first-order differential equation

If a differential equation is in this form $\frac{\mathrm{d}x}{\mathrm{d}t} = f(t)g(x)$, it's said to be a separable equation. To solve equations of this form, follow this procedure:

$$\frac{\mathrm{d}x}{\mathrm{d}t} = f(t)g(x) \Rightarrow \frac{\mathrm{d}x}{g(x)} = f(t)\,\mathrm{d}t \Rightarrow \int \frac{1}{g(x)}\,\mathrm{d}x = \int f(t)\,\mathrm{d}t \Rightarrow G(x) = C + F(t),$$

where $G(x)$ and $F(t)$ are the primitive functions of $g(x)$ and $f(t)$, respectively. Never forget the constant C in the above equation. This constant can be derived when the initial condition, i.e., $x(t = t_0) = x_0$, is given.

Linear one-variable first-order differential equation is in the form of $\frac{\mathrm{d}x}{\mathrm{d}t} + a(t)x = b(t)$. The solution is given by

$$x(t) = \mathrm{e}^{-\int a(t)\,\mathrm{d}t}\left[C + \int b(t)\,\mathrm{e}^{\int a(t)\,\mathrm{d}t}\,\mathrm{d}t\right].$$

A special case is that when $a(t)$, and/or $b(t)$, are constant. Specifically, observe the following two cases:

$$\frac{\mathrm{d}x}{\mathrm{d}t} + ax = b \Rightarrow x = C\mathrm{e}^{-at} + \frac{b}{a}$$

$$\frac{\mathrm{d}x}{\mathrm{d}t} + ax = b(t) \Rightarrow x = C\mathrm{e}^{-at} + \mathrm{e}^{-at}\int b(t)\mathrm{e}^{-at}\,\mathrm{d}t$$

For nonlinear differential equations, if they are or can be transformed into "exact" equations, then we can find the solutions to them. A nonlinear equation can be written in this form $f(t,x) + g(t,x)\frac{\mathrm{d}x}{\mathrm{d}t} = 0$ .If $f'_x(t,x) = g'_t(t,x)$, then the equation is called "exact." The solution of exact differential equation is given by the following equation

$$\int_{t_0}^{t} f(\tau, x)\,\mathrm{d}\tau + \int_{x_0}^{x} g(t_0, \zeta)\,\mathrm{d}\zeta = C.$$

If this condition is not met, the equation might be transformed into exact equations. To transform a equation into an exact equation, we need to find an appropriate $\beta(t,x)$ to multiply $f(t,x)$ and $g(t,x)$, so that $\frac{\mathrm{d}}{\mathrm{d}x}[\beta(t,x)f(t,x)] = \frac{\mathrm{d}}{\mathrm{d}t}[\beta(t,x)g(t,x)]$. This $\beta(t,x)$ is called the integrating factor. If the function happens to be in the following two cases, the integrating factor is easy to find. If $\frac{f'_x - g'_t}{g}$ is a function of t alone, then $\beta(t,x) = \mathrm{e}^{\int \frac{f'_x - g'_t}{g} \mathrm{d}t}$ .If $\frac{g'_t - f'_x}{f}$ is a function of t alone, then $\beta(t,x) = \mathrm{e}^{\int \frac{g'_t - f'_x}{f} \mathrm{d}x}$.

10.2.3 General method solving high order linear differential equations

The linear n th-order differential equations are in the form of

$$\frac{\mathrm{d}^n x}{\mathrm{d}t^n} + a_1(t)\frac{\mathrm{d}^{n-1}x}{\mathrm{d}t^{n-1}} + a_2(t)\frac{\mathrm{d}^{n-2}x}{\mathrm{d}t^{n-2}} + \dots + a_{n-1}(t)\frac{\mathrm{d}x}{\mathrm{d}t} + a_n(t)x = f(t). \qquad (10.1)$$

We call $\frac{\mathrm{d}^n x}{\mathrm{d}t^n} + \sum_{i=1}^{n} a_i(t)\frac{\mathrm{d}^{n-i}x}{\mathrm{d}t^{n-i}} = 0$ the homogeneous equation associated with Eq. (10.1). To solve Eq. (10.1), follow this procedure. First, find n general solutions for the homogeneous equation. Denote these solutions as $u_i(t)$, $i = 1,2,\dots,n$. Second, find a particular solution to Eq. (10.1). Denote this solution by $u^*(t)$. Then the general solutions to Eq. (10.1) are given by

$$x(t) = C_1u_1(t) + C_2u_2(t) + \dots + C_nu_n(t) + u^*(t),$$

for arbitrary constants $C_i,\ i = 1,2,\dots,n.$

It's not easy to find the solution $u_i(t)$ and $u^*(t)$ for general linear differential equations of high orders. However, when $a_i(t)$ are constants, then we can solve them in a systematic way. Formally, we are to solve

$$\frac{\mathrm{d}^n x}{\mathrm{d}t^n} + a_1\frac{\mathrm{d}^{n-1}x}{\mathrm{d}t^{n-1}} + a_2\frac{\mathrm{d}^{n-2}x}{\mathrm{d}t^{n-2}} + \dots + a_{n-1}\frac{\mathrm{d}x}{\mathrm{d}t} + a_nx = f(t). \qquad (10.2)$$

To find the general solutions for homogeneous equation associated with Eq. (10.2), we try to insert $x = \mathrm{e}^{rt}$ into Eq. (10.2) and equate $f(t)$ to zero. Observe that $\frac{\mathrm{d}^n}{\mathrm{d}t^n}\mathrm{e}^{rt} = r^n \mathrm{e}^{rt}$. So following this substitution, we have

$$r^n \mathrm{e}^{rt} + a_1 r^{n-1} \mathrm{e}^{rt} + a_2 r^{n-2} \mathrm{e}^{rt} + \ldots + a_{n-1} r \mathrm{e}^{rt} + a_n \mathrm{e}^{rt} = 0.$$

Or equivalently

$$p(r) = r^n + a_1 r^{n-1} + a_2 r^{n-2} + \ldots + a_{n-1} r + a_n = 0.$$

This is called the characteristic equation of the homogeneous equation associated with Eq. (10.2), and $p(r)$ is also known as characteristic polynomial. Obviously, if we solve Eq. (10.2), we can find the general solutions for the homogeneous equation. Denote the roots of Eq. (10.2) as $r_i, i = 1,2, \ldots, n$. If r_i is a distinct real root, then the corresponding solution to the homogeneous differential equation is $\mathrm{e}^{r_i t}$. If r_i is a real root with multiplicity m, then the corresponding solutions to the homogeneous differential equation are $\mathrm{e}^{r_i t}$, $t\,\mathrm{e}^{r_i t}$,..., $t^{m-1}\,\mathrm{e}^{r_i t}$. If r_i is a pair of complex roots $r = \alpha + i\beta$ and $\hat{r} = \alpha - i\beta$, then the corresponding solutions are $\mathrm{e}^{\alpha t}\cos\beta t$ and $\mathrm{e}^{\alpha t}\sin\beta t$. If r_i is a pair of complex roots with multiplicity m, then the corresponding solutions are $\mathrm{e}^{\alpha t}\cos\beta t$, $\mathrm{e}^{\alpha t}\sin\beta t$, ... , $t^{m-1}\,\mathrm{e}^{\alpha t}\cos\beta t$, $t^{m-1}\,\mathrm{e}^{\alpha t}\sin\beta t$.

To find a particular solution to Eq. (10.2), try the method of undetermined coefficients or the method of variation of parameters. The method of variation of parameters is more general despite the form of $f(t)$ in Eq. (10.2). The procedure is as follows. First define the general solution to Eq. (10.2) as

$$x = C_1(t)u_1(t) + \ldots + C_n u_n(t),$$

where ui(t) are the general solutions to the homogeneous differential equation. Then construct the following system of equations:

$$\sum_{i=1}^{n}\left(\left[\frac{\mathrm{d}}{\mathrm{d}t}C_i(t)\right]u_i(t)\right) = 0$$

$$\sum_{i=1}^{n}\left(\left[\frac{\mathrm{d}}{\mathrm{d}t}C_i(t)\right]\left[\frac{\mathrm{d}}{\mathrm{d}t}u_i(t)\right]\right) = 0$$

$$\sum_{i=1}^{n}\left(\left[\frac{d}{dt}C_i(t)\right]\left[\frac{d^2}{dt^2}u_i(t)\right]\right) = 0$$

$$\vdots$$

$$\sum_{i=1}^{n}\left(\left[\frac{d}{dt}C_i(t)\right]\left[\frac{d^{n-2}}{dt^{n-2}}u_i(t)\right]\right) = 0$$

$$\sum_{i=1}^{n}\left(\left[\frac{d}{dt}C_i(t)\right]\left[\frac{d^{n-1}}{dt^{n-1}}u_i(t)\right]\right) = f(t).$$

This system of equations can be solved recursively, therefore we can find all the $C_i(t)$, and thus the general solution to Eq. (10.2).

The method of undetermined coefficients is less laborious than the method of variation of parameters.

10.3 Fixed point

Fixed point is important when we discuss the existence of equilibrium. The idea of fixed point is that applying the mapping of f to the fixed point yields the point itself. If the system is defined by a function $f: \mathbb{R}^n \to \mathbb{R}^m$, then the fixed points of this function are candidates for equilibrium. For instance, Nash equilibrium of a two-player game requires the strategy actions (a_i, a_{-i}) as mutually best responses. In words, it requires $f_1(a_1, a_2) = f_2(a_1, a_2)$. Fixed point theories are helpful when we discuss the existence of the pair (a_i, a_{-i}). Observe that $f_1(a_1, a_2) = f_2(a_1, a_2)$ can be rewritten as $f_1(a_1, a_2) - f_2(a_1, a_2) = 0$, or $f_1(a_1, a_2) - f_2(a_1, a_2) + (a_1, a_2) = a_1, a_2$. If we define $F(a_1, a_2) = f_1(a_1, a_2) - f_2(a_1, a_2) + (a_1, a_2)$, then the equilibrium boils down to find the fixed point of $F(a_1, a_2)$.

Theorem 10.1. *If* χ *is a non-empty compact set, then function* $f: \mathcal{X} \to \mathcal{X}$ *has at least one fixed point.*

This theorem is also known as **Brouwer's Fixed Point Theorem.**

After finding the fixed point(s), we are usually interested in the stability of these points. Let $\bar{x}$ be the fixed point of system of difference equations $x_{t+1} = f(x_t)$. Using linear approximation, we can rewrite this difference equation as $x_{t+1} = f(\bar{x}) + f'(\bar{x})(x - \bar{x})$. By definition, $f(\bar{x}) = \bar{x}$. So $x_{t+1} - \bar{x} = f'(\bar{x})(x - \bar{x})$, and furthermore $|x_{t+1} - \bar{x}| = |f'(\bar{x})||(x - \bar{x})|$. If the fixed point $\bar{x}$ is locally stable, then x_{t+1} must be closer to $\bar{x}$ than is x_t . Hence local stability requires $|f'(\bar{x})| < 1$.

We can restate the above property without using linear approximation. Local stability requires that $\left|\frac{\mathrm{d}(x_{t+1} - \bar{x})}{\mathrm{d}(x_t - \bar{x})}\right| < 1$, i.e., when x_t gets away from $\bar{x}$,

x_{t+1} gets closer to $\bar{x}$. Since $\frac{\mathrm{d}(x_{t+1}-\bar{x})}{\mathrm{d}(x_t-\bar{x})}=\frac{\mathrm{d}x_{t+1}}{\mathrm{d}x_t}=f'(\bar{x})$ in the neighborhood of $\bar{x}$. So local stability requires $|f'(\bar{x})|<1$. If $f(x_t)$ .is linear, for instance, $f(x_t)=ax_t+b$, then $\frac{\mathrm{d}x_{t+1}}{\mathrm{d}x_t}=a$. Then there is only one fixed point—the origin point. $|a|<1$ implies this fixed point is globally stable.

Similarly, if $\bar{x}$ is the fixed point of system of differential equations $\frac{\mathrm{d}x}{\mathrm{d}t}=f(x)=f(\bar{x})+f'(\bar{x})(x-\bar{x})$, so due to $\frac{\mathrm{d}\bar{x}}{\mathrm{d}t}=f(\bar{x})=0$, we have $\frac{\mathrm{d}x}{\mathrm{d}t}=f'(\bar{x})(x-\bar{x})$. By definition, local stability requires $\frac{\mathrm{d}x}{\mathrm{d}t}<0$ when $x>\bar{x}$, and $\frac{\mathrm{d}x}{\mathrm{d}t}>0$ when $x<\bar{x}$. So $f'(\bar{x})<0$.

Overall, the above can be generalized into the following theorem with respect to the **Stability of Fixed Points**.

Theorem 10.2. *If the difference equation* $f\colon x_t\in\mathbb{R}\to x_{t+1}\in\mathbb{R}$ *has a fixed point* $\bar{x}$ *, then* $\bar{x}$ *is locally stable when* $|f'(\bar{x})|<1$ *and is locally (and therefore globally) unstable when* $|f'(\bar{x})|>1$ *. And if f is a linear function, then* $\bar{x}$ *is unique and globally stable if it is locally stable.*

If the difference equation $f\colon \mathbf{x}_t\in\mathbb{R}^n\to\mathbf{x}_{t+1}\in\mathbb{R}^n$ *has a fixed point* $\bar{\mathbf{x}}$ *, then*

1. when the difference equation is linear—hence having a Matrix representation, say **A**—$\bar{\mathbf{x}}$ *is globally stable if the absolute value of all the eigenvalues of* **A** *are smaller than 1, otherwise* $\bar{\mathbf{x}}$ *is globally unstable. And when* **I**—**A** *is nonsingular,* $\bar{\mathbf{x}}$ *is the unique fixed point.*

2. when the difference equation is nonlinear, $\bar{\mathbf{x}}$ *is locally stable if the absolute value of all the eigenvalues of the Jacobian matrix of* $f(\bar{\mathbf{x}})$ *are smaller than 1, otherwise* $\bar{\mathbf{x}}$ *is globally unstable.*

The above theorem deals with difference equation. The Theorem for differential equation is the following.

Theorem 10.3. *If the differential equation is* $\frac{\mathrm{d}x_t}{\mathrm{d}t}=f(x_t)$ *in* $\mathbb{R}$ *, and* $\bar{x}$ *is the fixed point, then* $\bar{x}$ *is locally stable when* $f'(\bar{x})<0$ *and is locally (and therefore globally) unstable when* $f'(\bar{x})>0$.

If the differential equation is $\nabla_t \mathbf{x}_t = f(\mathbf{x}_t)$ *in* $\mathbb{R}^n$ *, and* $\bar{\mathbf{x}}$ *is the fixed point, then*

1. when the differential equation is linear—hence having a Matrix representation, say $\mathbf{A}$*—*$\bar{\mathbf{x}}$ *is globally stable if all the eigenvalues of* $\mathbf{A}$ *are distinct and negative, otherwise* $\bar{\mathbf{x}}$ *is globally unstable.*

2. when the differential equation is nonlinear, $\bar{\mathbf{x}}$ *is locally stable if all the eigenvalues of the Jacobian matrix of* $f(\bar{\mathbf{x}})$ *are distinct and negative, otherwise* $\bar{\mathbf{x}}$ *is globally unstable.*

10.4 Static optimization

The objective function is real-valued in most economic research, because when we compare the results of different choices it is unclear how to compare multidimensional results. For instance, net profit is a good objective function. In portfolio choice, we care about both return and risk. Any portfolio choice generates a result that has these two dimensions. We can't compare such results directly. So we have to define a utility function—which is obviously a real-valued function. So in this chapter, the objective functions are all real-valued.

First notice the following theorem (10.4).

Theorem 10.4. *If* $f: \mathcal{X} \to \mathbb{R}$ *is continuous on a compact set* $\mathcal{X}$ *, then both global maximum and minimum exist.*

This theorem is also known as **Weierstrass Theorem**.

A general maximization problem can be defined as follows. The objective function $f: \mathbb{R}^n \to \mathbb{R}$.

$$\max_x f(x) \qquad subject\ to: g_i(x) \le c_i, for\ i = 1,2,\ldots \tag{10.3}$$

The general approach to solve Eq. (10.3) is to solve the following functions.

$$\nabla f(x) = \sum \lambda_i \nabla g_i(x)$$

For all $i: \lambda_i \ge 0, \quad g_i(x) - c_i \le 0, \quad \lambda_i(g(x) - c_i) = 0$

Notice that there is an important trick where $\frac{\partial f}{\partial x_i}$ is not a function of x_i . In this case, the problem imposes no necessary requirement on the choice of x_i , so just ignore x_i from the above equation. Then consider the boundary points of x_i .

The Kuhn-Tucker Theorem discusses the similar maximization problem as Eq. (10.3), except that it requires $x \gg 0$. Formally, The Kuhn-Tucker Theorem discusses the following maximization problem.

$$\max_{x} f(x) \qquad subject\ to: g_i(x) \le c_i, and\ x_i > 0, for\ i = 1,2,\dots \tag{10.4}$$

To solve Eq. (10.4), solve the following functions.

For all *i*:

$$\begin{cases} x_i \ge 0 \\ \dfrac{\partial f(x)}{\partial x_i} - \sum_i \lambda_i \dfrac{\partial g_i(x)}{\partial x_i} \le 0 \\ x_i \left(\dfrac{\partial f(x)}{\partial x_i} - \sum_i \lambda_i \dfrac{\partial g_i(x)}{\partial x_i} \right) = 0 \end{cases}$$

and

$$\begin{cases} \lambda_i \ge 0 \\ g_i(x) \le 0 \\ \lambda_i (g_i(x) - c_i) = 0 \end{cases}$$

Notice that in the above maximization problems, we usually assume that the objective function $f(x)$ is a real valued function.

10.5 Duality

After we find the optimum $\mathbf{x}^*$ to problem (10.3), we are often interested in the optimal value function. Let $\phi(\mathbf{x}^*, \mathbf{a})$ be the optimal value function for a maximization problem, where $\mathbf{x}^*$ is the optimal choice and $\mathbf{a}$ is the parameters of the problem. Similarly, let us define $\varphi(\mathbf{x}^*, \mathbf{a})$ as the optimal value function for a maximization problem. Then we have the following theorem.

Theorem 10.5. Let $\phi(x^*, a)$ and $\varphi(x^*, a)$ be the optimal value function for maximization and minimization problem, respectively, where is the parameters of the problem. Then:

1. *if* $f(\mathbf{x}^*, \mathbf{a})$ *is convex in* $\mathbf{a}$ *, then* $\phi(\mathbf{x}^*, \mathbf{a})$ *is also convex in* $\mathbf{a}$ *;*

2. *if* $f(\mathbf{x}^*, \mathbf{a})$ *is concave in* $\mathbf{a}$ *, then* $\varphi(\mathbf{x}^*, \mathbf{a})$ *is also concave in* $\mathbf{a}$ *;*

3. *if* $f(\mathbf{x}^*, \mathbf{a})$ *is linear in* $\mathbf{a}$ *, then* $\phi(\mathbf{x}^*, \mathbf{a})$ *is convex in* $\mathbf{a}$ *, and* $\varphi(\mathbf{x}^*, \mathbf{a})$ *is concave in* $\mathbf{a}$ *.*

Also notice the following property.

$$\nabla_{\mathrm{a}} \mathbf{x}^*(\mathbf{a}) = \nabla_{\mathrm{a}}^2 \phi(\mathbf{x}^*, \mathbf{a})$$

In the above equation, notice that x^* is the function of $\mathbf{a}$. The left hand side of the equation is the Jacobian matrix of $\mathrm{x}^*(\mathrm{a})$, and the right hand side is the Hessian matrix of optimal value function $\phi(\mathrm{x}^*, \mathrm{a})$.

Chapter 11
Empirical methodology

11.1 Regressions

11.1.1 Simple regressions

Sometimes the estimates of the coefficient are too large or too small. And direct comparison of coefficients may be not really meaningful. So we can scale the coefficient by the standard deviation of the corresponding variables, and interpret the scaled coefficients as how much one standard deviation change in the corresponding variable results in the change in the dependent variable. Notice the scaled coefficient is the product of the original coefficients and the standard deviation. This way of scaling coefficients also facilitates the (loose) comparison of explanatory power across the independent variables.

For OLS regressions, one concern is the heteroscedasticity of error terms. If the error terms change across observations, then the standard errors may be biased. To account for this problem, we should use heteroscedasticity consistent or white standard errors. Clustered standard errors are robust to heteroscedasticity (footnote 4 of Petersen, 2009, p. 438).

Probit and Logit regressions are usually estimated using the maximum likelihood method, because the OLS is inappropriate due the nonlinear nature of these regressions. An additional advantage of maximum likelihood method is that the heteroskedasticity is automatically accounted for. The difference between logit and probit regressions is that logit regression assumes logistic distribution whereas probit follows normal distribution.

When the dependent variable of interest is the number of times an event occurs, count regression should be used. Liu (2009, pp. 116–117) provides a discussion of the econometric details.

11.1.2 Regression discontinuity

Lee and Lemieux (2010, p. 287) states the key assumption of a valid RD design: "all other factors determining Y must be evolving 'smoothly' with respect to X". See also Papay et al. (2011), while an example in finance is Chava and Roberts (2008).

But when using regression discontinuity, we need to keep in mind the following limitations and cautions. If the cutoff point is extremely high or low, then the RD result says nothing about the treatment effect on the extremely low or high subjects. For example, consider the case in which the treatment is a scholarship award, which is based on the exam results of the students. If the student is not rewarded a scholarship unless he gets 90 percent or higher in the exam, then the RD results shows the effect of this scholarship on the student's future academic achievement, but this is the effect on the subpopulation of smartest students. If we believe this effect varies among smarter and less smart students, it will be inappropriate to generalize the RD results to the effect on less smart students. So when the threshold of rewarding a scholarship is 50 percent in the exam, this is not a big concern. In summary, RD measures the effect of treatment on the population around the threshold. To what extent we can generalize the estimated effect to the whole population depends on what extent we are willing to assume the effect is homogeneous among the population.

11.1.3 Ordered probit regression

Ordered probit regression applies to linear regressions with discrete dependent variables. Binary choices and multiple choices are obviously discrete variables. But ordered probit regression goes beyond these cases. In microstructure studies, transaction prices are discrete, and the discreteness has a large effect on stocks with lower prices. So we can use ordered probit regression rather than OLS to account for the discreteness.

Hausman et al. (1992) discuss the ideas of using ordered probit regression to study the price change. Suppose the observable price changes are Z_k . Because prices are only quoted at integer multiples of tick, so Z_k is discrete. Suppose there is a "true" price change sequence that is not subject to the price quotation requirement, denoted as Z_k^* . We want to estimate $Z_k^* = \boldsymbol{\beta}'\mathbf{x}_k + \boldsymbol{\epsilon}_k$, where $\mathbf{x}_k$ is the vector of exogenous variables that affect the price change. A mapping from unobservable Z_k^* to observable Z_k is given by

$$Z_k = \begin{cases} s_1 & \text{if} \quad Z_k^* \in A_1 \equiv (-\infty, \alpha_1], \\ s_2 & \text{if} \quad Z_k^* \in A_2 \equiv (\alpha_1, \alpha_2], \\ \vdots & \vdots \\ s_m & \text{if} \quad Z_k^* \in A_m \equiv (\alpha_{m-1}, \infty]. \end{cases} \tag{11.1}$$

So $\mathbb{P}(Z_k = s_i|\mathbf{x}_k) = \mathbb{P}(Z_k^* \in A_i|\mathbf{x}_k) = \mathbb{P}(\boldsymbol{\beta}'\mathbf{x}_k + \epsilon_k \in A_i|\mathbf{x}_k)$. If we assume ϵ_k follows INID normal distribution, then we have the following:[1]

$$\mathbb{P}(Z_k = s_i|\mathbf{x}_k) = \begin{cases} \Phi\left(\frac{\alpha_1 - \boldsymbol{\beta}'\mathbf{x}_k}{\sigma_k}\right) & \text{if} \quad i = 1, \\ \Phi\left(\frac{\alpha_i - \boldsymbol{\beta}'\mathbf{x}_k}{\sigma_k}\right) - \Phi\left(\frac{\alpha_{i-1} - \boldsymbol{\beta}'\mathbf{x}_k}{\sigma_k}\right) & \text{if} \quad 1 < i < m, \\ 1 - \Phi\left(\frac{\alpha_{m-1} - \boldsymbol{\beta}'\mathbf{x}_k}{\sigma_k}\right) & \text{if} \quad i = m. \end{cases} \tag{11.1}$$

where $\Phi(\cdot)$ is the standard normal cumulative distribution function.

The implementation of an ordered probit regression entails the following steps. Define the boundaries. If the dependent variable is multiple choices, the boundaries are simply the integers representing each choice. If the dependent variable is the discrete prices, the boundaries may be integer times of the tick or other price rounding unit. In latter case, use the empirical distribution of the dependent variable to find the appropriate boundaries. Try to balance the needs of price resolution and the number of parameters to be estimated.

11.1.4 Vector autoregression

A vector autoregression (VAR) analysis studies the relations among dependent

1 INID stands for independent and NOT identical distributed. It allows (conditional) heteroscedasticity in .

variables along their time path. Sometimes independent variables also appear in the models. The independent variables are exogenous to the system of interest, and they appear in none of the equations as a dependent variable. Thereby, the number of dependent (endogenous) variables should equal the number of the equations.

Conventionally, VAR analyses are applied to time-series data. We can also conduct VAR to panel data. For example, a time-series VAR may study the interrelation between GDP and employment rate. A VAR for panel data may study the interrelation between institutional ownership and stock returns, but for a panel of stocks rather than a particular stock. For panel data, we compute the average of coefficient estimates, without reporting the significance. But we know the significance for each individual time-series, so we can report the percentage of time-series (stocks for example) with positive and negative coefficients that are significantly different from 0 at conventional confidence level, say five percent.

Table IV of Griffin et al. (2003, p. 2299) provides an example of VAR models.

11.1.5 Panel data regressions

Petersen (2009) reviews how recently published papers deal with panel data. Besides OLS without any adjustment, the following three approaches are popular: FamaMacBeth procedure (Fama and MacBeth, 1973), OLS with adjusted standard error, and fixed effect dummy regression.

For the regression $\mathbf{y} = \mathbf{X}\boldsymbol{\beta} + \boldsymbol{\epsilon}$, its OLS estimate is $\widehat{\boldsymbol{\beta}} = (\mathbf{X}'\mathbf{X})^{-1}\mathbf{X}'\mathbf{y}$.

There are two ways to adjust OLS standard errors: clustered standard errors and (modified) Newey-West adjusted standard errors. Notably, these two ways adjust OLS standard errors, with OLS coefficients unchanged: "[Newey-West procedure] was initially designed to account a serial correlation of unknown form in the residuals of a single time series" (Petersen, 2009, p. 452). This procedure has been modified to adjust OLS standard errors. When computing NeweyWest standard errors, it needs to specify the lag of autocorrelation. In panel data, the lag can be set as the maximum time periods minus one.

We need to consider the following three questions: 1) Is there a firm effect or time effect or both? 2) Is the firm effect permanent or temporary? 3) Is the time effect constant or non-constant? Firm effect: the residuals of a given firm are autocorrelated (time-series dependence). Time effect: the residuals of a given year are correlated across different firms (cross-sectional dependence) (Petersen,

2009, p. 436). The firm effect is temporary if it dies away over time. The non-constant time effect means that a shock happened in a specific year has a larger impact on some firms while a smaller impact on others. Including time dummies removes all constant time effect, so if clustering with time dimension changes the standard error when time dummies are included, it indicates a nonconstant time effect (Petersen, 2009, p. 470). Similarly, including firm dummies removes all permanent firm effect.

Table 11.1: Suggested methods for firm and/or time effect.

This table is how to deal with firm and/or time effect in panel data. The suggestion mainly comes from Petersen (2009).

Effect	Methods
Only firm effect	Permanent cluster by firm, or include firm dummies temporary cluster by firm
Only time effect	Fama-MacBeth generally works. Clustering by time works only with large number of time periods
Both	Include dummies for one dimension (the dimension that has a small number of clusters), then cluster by the other. If both dimensions have large number of clusters, then clustering by both also works.

The suggested way to account for the firm and/or time effect is the following.

Random effect and fixed effect traditionally mean the effect is a random variable or a parameter to be estimated. However, a more relevant view should be they refer to the unobserved effect as uncorrelated or correlated with observed explanatory variables. If the unobserved effect is uncorrelated with explanatory variables, i.e., it is random effect, then a pooled OLS treatment is appropriate for panel data. In contrast, when the unobserved effect is fixed effect, pooled OLS is biased and inconsistent.

Generally speaking, two situations invalidate using pooled OLS. One is the serial dependence of explanatory variables; the other is the correlation between explanatory variables and unobserved effects. An extreme example of the first situation is using the lagged dependent variable as explanatory variable.

For random effects, pooled OLS often suffices. Nevertheless, to account for the serial dependence of explanatory variables, GLS is more appropriate.

Most of the financial data are panel data. When dealing with panel data, researchers often control firm effect and/or year effect. These effects are more formally known as **fixed effect**. Fixed effect is not aimed for processing panel data only. It has more broader usage. Fixed effect is aimed to control for *unobservable* *effect*. Obviously we can't incorporate every factors into our regressions, partly because we don't know what they are, and partly because we don't have the data on some factors. This inability compromises the explanatory power of the regressions. To solve this *unobservable factor problem*, we can control for *fixed effect*. For example, we know that some unobservable firm characteristics (denoted as $\mathbf{u}$) may determine the firms's behaviors (measured by $\mathbf{y}$). If we are willing to assume that these unobservable firm characteristics do not vary over time, then by differencing $\mathbf{y} = \alpha + \boldsymbol{\beta}\mathbf{x} + \boldsymbol{\gamma}\mathbf{u} + \mathbf{v} + \boldsymbol{\epsilon}$, we cancel out the term $\boldsymbol{\gamma}\mathbf{u}$. That is the idea of fixed effect. If a firm has more than two observations, which is always true, we *difference* them by adding a series of time dummies.

With firm fixed effects in regressions, the coefficients represent, or are mainly driven by, the *within firm* variations. With year fixed effects in regressions, the coefficients represent, or are mainly driven by, the *across firm* variations.

In most cases, fixed effects are something that we want to control, so we seldom report the coefficients of the dummies of the fixed effects. Bao and Edmans (2011), however, provide an example in which we are actually interested in these coefficients. The problem they are address is: are the "quality" of advising banks related with different M&A deal returns? In other words, is it true that some banks systematically outperform other banks in terms of providing better advising services to their clients? The challenge this problem imposes is how to measure the quality of investment banks. Some researchers use market share or reputation. But these metrics are imperfect proxies. So unsurprisingly they find no significant relations between investment bank quality and M&A deal returns. Bao and Edmans (2011) use fixed effect to explore if there are systematic variations among banks in the first place. The second paragraph on p. 2296 details the estimation of the fixed effects models, results of which are reported in Table 3 on the next page. The fixed effects are simply the dummies for each banks. The coefficients for these dummies measure the "quality" of the banks. By doing so, the authors avoid the challenge of how to measure the quality.

11.2 Non-regression methods

Equality test is arguably the most widely used empirical research method other than regressions. First we need to decide whether we are comparing paired observations or two samples. A comparison of paired observations could be comparing whether the firm's performance changes before and after an event. In this case, we "pair" same firms. In contrast, there is no such paired relation when we do two sample comparison. For example, we may want test if the government owned firms have same percentage of independent directors as do private owned firms. The second thing we should decide before we do the test is what we are testing. Are we testing the equality of location—i.e., mean or median, or the equality of spread—i.e., the interquartile range because variance is usually hard to quantify. The third thing is to decide what distribution we are willing to assume for the data.

The following table details the tests designed for these cases.

Portfolio construction is another great way to test hypotheses in finance research. Constructing portfolios and comparing the characteristics across the portfolios provide crude evidence that A causes B. Specifically, we first sort observations on A to construct portfolios, then we compare the average of B across portfolios. One critique to this method is that A might be correlated with other factors, and these factors might be the true determinants of B. Lemmon et al. (2008, last two paragraphs on p. 1582) provide an example of dealing with this critique. They first regress A on these factors, and then sort the residuals of the regressions to construct portfolios. By showing the results agree with that of the portfolios sorted on A, we defend our claim that A is the true determinant of B. Furthermore, if the regressors are the determinants, the divergence of B across portfolios sorted on residuals should be much smaller than that of portfolios sorted on A, and the divergence should disappear over time very quickly since the divergence is caused by random shocks. See Liu and Strong (2008) for how to calculate the buy-and-hold return without incurring large rebalancing costs.

Table 11.2: Equality test methods

This table details the equality test methods. The content comes from Paul A. Pappas and Venita DePuy's note An *Overview of Non-parametric Tests in SAS: When, Why, and How.*

Paired vs.2-sample	Test	Test what	Distribution assumptions	Other comments
Paired	Paired T-test	Equality of the mean	Observations are independently, identically, normally distributed.	
	Sign Test and Signed Rank Test	Equality of the median	Observations are independently and symmetrically distributed. The observations do not need to have identical distributions, nor do they have identical distributions.	Non-parametric test. If the data contain outliers or come from fattailed distribution, use sign test; otherwise use signed rank test.
2-sample	T-test	Equality of mean or variance	Observations are independently, normally distributed.	A equality test of variance will be conducted. And the test of equal mean has two results, one is under the assumption of equal variance, the other is under the assumption of unequal variance.
	Wilcoxon Rank Sum Test	Equality of the median	The null hypothesis is the two samples are identically distributed. The alternative hypothesis is that they differ only with respect to the median. In other words, we have to assume that the two samples have the same shape and spread.	Non-parametric test. Without using EXACT option, only approximate test will conducted. Approximate test becomes unreliable when sample size has any of the following features: small, skewed, fat-tailed. Exact test, however, may take a long time to perform.
	Ansari-Bradley Test	Equality of the spread given identical center	Observations are independent, and two samples have same medians. In other words, we have to assume that the two samples have the same shape and median.	Non-parametric test.
	Kolmogorov-Smirnov Test	The overall the distributions are identical	Two samples are independent.	If we are willing to assume the assumptions in the above two rows, the above tests are more powerful.

Variance decomposition helps us to compare the relative importance of determinant. Lemmon et al. (2008, p. 1588) provides an example. When conducting such analyses, it is helpful to first try firm effect and year effect. If the firm effect has larger R^2 than year effect, then the variation is more due to the time invariant factors. The following papers also use principal components to study the common factors in liquidity (Corwin and Lipson, 2011; Hasbrouck and Seppi,

2001; Korajczyk and Sadka, 2008).

11.3 Endogeneity

The fundamental reason of endogeneity is omitted variables. These variables are omitted either because they are unobservable or unmeasurable, or because we are not aware of them. The omitted variables might be the true force driving the dependent variables. Or the omitted variables are correlated with the residuals, so the estimates are biased. Another reason of endogeneity is the inter-dependence of dependent variables. For example, the supply and demand. In this case, we assume that we know the casual relations among the variables. But omitted variables is a more fundamental reason for endogeneity, because even though we know there is inter-dependence among variables, we cannot rule out the possibility of omitted variables.

Endogeneity has the following symptoms/causes: omitted variable, simultaneity, reverse causality, and measurement errors. Omitted variable is to some extent similar to simultaneity, but not completely the same. Omitted variable may be the true reason behind both dependent and independent variables, so in this case, it's not that the independent variable causes the dependent variable, but rather the omitted variable that causes such. Another scenario of simultaneity is that the dependent and independent variables determine each other, like the demand and supply. Measurement errors arise when we have imperfect proxy of the variable of interest. When the measurement errors happen for the dependent variable, OLS estimates are unbiased as long as the measurement error is uncorrelated with explanatory variables, while the measurement errors for independent variables do cause bias. Reverse causality arises when the dependent variable determines independent variables, rather than the reverse. For example, the more firemen fighting the fire, the bigger the fire is. But we can't say firemen cause fire, although they are highly correlated and unsurprisingly regression of fire on the number of firemen gives good statistics. So, reverse causality often arises when the dependent and independent variables are of the same period. Since the cause must precede the outcome in the timeline, we often include lag variables in regressors to address reverse causality.

Notice that it's almost impossible to completely rule out endogeneity, because we can never be one hundred percent sure we've controlled for all relevant variables, not to even mention the "right" function forms. So any critique on endogenous problems should be story-based. That is, the critique should first work out a story indicating that the other variables determine the dependent variable.

The following methods address endogeneity, but they have their weakness as well.

11.3.1 Natural experiment

A natural experiment helps establish a casual relationship between variables. Suppose we have found the following correlation:

$$Y = \alpha + \beta_1 X_1 + \beta_2 X_2 + \epsilon \tag{11.3}$$

We want to further show that X_2 does have a casual effect on Y. For concreteness, suppose $\beta_2 > 0$. If there is an exogenous event which increases X_2, then an increase in Y after the event supports this casual effect of X_2 on Y.

An exogenous shock provides a natural experiment. For example, a new regulation is imposed so that every firm should increase the proportion of independent directors. This shock is exogenous because the introduction of this regulation has little connection with the firm's characteristics. Since all the firms are "forced" to increase the proportion of independent directors, this change is not the result of the firm's self-selection, thus it is not endogenous. In this case, we know the reason of the change in proportion of independent directors, that is, the exogenous regulation change. Therefore, omitted variables are not serious concerns. Furthermore, since all the firms are subject to the same exogenous shock, we do not even need to control it.

Clean natural experiments are actually rare. We need to check and address the following issues which potentially undermine the explanatory power of our natural experiment. First check if the exogenous shock also directly or indirectly changes the dependent variable. If it does, this experiment is possibly worthless. For example, in the recent financial crisis, governments set upper limit on CEO compensations, so firms may pay their CEOs less. But given that this regulation is introduced in a financial crisis, when almost all the firms had difficult times, firms tend to lower the CEO compensations even without this regulation. Therefore, this regulation is not a good natural experiment. In contrast, the above example of independent directors is a good natural experiment because the exogenous regulation change is unlikely to directly change the firm performance.

The second issue to check is whether there are other events happening. The third issue is the "self-selection" issue. Take the above experiment of independent director regulation, we need to ask why some firms have "sufficient" independent directors even before the regulation change? This question is exactly the self-selection issue.

11.3.2 Difference approach

One limitation of difference approach is that there is no perfect match. Of course this is not a problem if we match firms with themselves. But matching with themselves has another problem: why do these firms change in the first place? There might still be omitted variables.

Firm fixed effect is also in essence a difference approach. It assumes that the unobserved firm characteristics remain constant over time. If this assumption fails to hold, firm fixed effect is problematic. And this assumption is very likely to be violated when we are analyzing firms with long histories. Furthermore, whenever we are dealing with long histories, we should be concerned about trend.

11.3.3 Instrumental variables

Instrumental variable is correlated with the explanatory variables, but uncorrelated with independent variables. We first regress the explanatory variable on instrumental variable. By so doing, we "purge" the explanatory variable. Then we use the purged explanatory variable in the regression. Distance is often a candidate for an instrumental variable.

A perfect instrumental variable should be generated by a random coin-flip. If there is a lottery or biological process (for example, gender determination of a baby) behind the instrumental variable, this is perfect.

11.3.4 Simultaneous equations

The above approaches deal with the endogeneity due to omitted variables. For the endogeneity due to inter-dependence of variables, we can use simultaneous equations. But when using this method, we implicitly assume the casual relations among variables, and this method says little about the endogeneity due to omitted variables.

11.3.5 Self-selection and Heckman model

Krishnan et al. (2011, pp. 1314–1317) implement a standard Heckman (1979) two step selection procedure.

Hoechle et al. (2012, Section 3.4 on p. 52) implement a Heckman (1979) model.

The Heckman model addresses the following question. Suppose we observe two characteristics of firms, A and B. We want to test if characteristic B affects the firm value. But it is possible that firms with characteristic A tend to choose characteristic B. If it is the case, we cannot say characteristic B affects firm value, rather it is characteristic A that affects firm value. To rule out A's effect on the firm value, we run a Heckman model. The Heckman model consists of two steps. The first step estimates a probit model of firm's choice of B. The inverse Mills ratio from this probit model enters the regression in the second step as an explanatory variable.

The GMM model accounts for the dynamic endogeneity. See Hoechle et al. (2012, Section 3.4.2 on p. 55), and Wintoki, Linck, and Netter (forthcoming JFE) for detailed discussion.

Equation 10 of Li and Prabhala (2007, p. 44) shows that the self-selection can be viewed as a omitted variable problem. Then they proceed to interpret the inverse Mills ratio term as the private information explaining the firm's choice.

11.3.6 Smart experimental designs getting around endogeneity

Masulis and Mobbs (2011) study the inside directors sitting on the board of other firms. They show that most of such inside directors begin with single directorship in the home firm. Then after several years, they become directors of other firms. So appointment of such inside directors at the beginning is not endogenous at all.

Masulis et al. (2011) study the percentage of foreign directors. They use the distance of the firm's headquarter from a major international airport as an instrumental variable. This instrumental variable is obviously correlated with the number of foreign directors. But we can reasonably assume that this distance plays no role in determining the firm's performance.

Knyazeva et al. (2009) use the supply of directors as an instrumental variable. The supply of directors is measured by how many firms are near the headquarters of the firm, because most of the directors are the senior executives of other firms.

And since a firm's headquarters is chosen long before the firm chooses directors, the location of the headquarters can be viewed as an exogenous variable.

11.3.7 When should we be concerned about endogeneity

We should always be concerned about endogeneity. But the following examples indicate endogeneity might be a serious problem.

Suppose we want to show $y = \alpha+\beta x+\beta_0 x_0 + \epsilon$. If x assumes only discrete values—for example, binary values—then we can divide the samples into several groups according to x. It might be helpful to check if there are differences in the explanatory variables x. If the differences are very significant for most of the explanatory variables, we should be concerned that these different groups of samples come from a totally different "world." What we would like to see is that the differences are insignificant, because the insignificance of the differences indicates that the firms are very similar, except that they have different x. Therefore we can claim that the samples are "allocated" into these groups randomly. On the contrary, if we find the differences are significant, we should ask ourselves: why do samples with particular characteristics in x_0 enter the particular group? In other words, why do some samples end up with a particular value of x, while others do not? This question casts serious doubt on whether the explanatory variable x_0 are really exogenous. If they are not, then an endogenous problem exists.

11.3.8 Other research design issues

Convergence is sometimes the key research question. Lemmon et al. (2008) discuss the convergences of the firm's leverage over time, i.e., high (low) levered firms tend to decrease (increase) their leverage. To illustrate this convergence, they plot the average leverage of four portfolios sorted on initial their leverage (see Fig. 1 on p. 1580). The caption of the figure details how to generate the plot. Notice they also plots the 90% confidence interval around the averages. Another issue is **bounded support**. Because leverage ratios, by definition, are bounded within unity interval, it might be unsurprising if we find firms with extreme leverages tend to revert to the some moderate levels. To examine this possibility, the authors propose a logitistic transformation of the leverage ratios, so that the transformed leverages are unbounded. Recall that a logistic transformation maps $x \in [0,1]$ to $\ln[x/(1-x)]$, which can be infinitely (positively) large. However, the logistic transformation is undefined when x is either 0 or 1. So one remedy to this limitation is simply ingnore these observations provided they consist of only a small portion. Another remedy is to add a small number, say 0.001, to these observations.

Very often the time, our empirical research tries to compare factors. Suppose we have known that $Y = \alpha + \beta_1 X_1 + \beta_2 X_2 + \beta_3 X_3 + \epsilon$, i.e., three factors X_1, X_2, X_3 affect Y. Sometimes we are interested in the relative importance of these factors on Y. There are several ways to do this: variance decomposition, comparing the coefficients βs scaled by the standard deviation of the corresponding Xs, and compute the "hypothetical" value of Y. Guo et al. (2011, p. 503) provide an example for the third method.

11.4 Measurements

11.4.1 Sample and data

The first thing that we need to take seriously is whether the sample has survivorship bias. Lemmon et al. (2008, p. 1581) not only discuss the whole sample and survivors, they also discuss the firms that ceased to exist. Another way to mitigate the effect of listing and delisting of firms is to randomly choose a fixed number of firms for each period (see Bhattacharya and Galpin, 2011, p. 748).

As for industry classification Fama and French (1997) propose a 48 industry classification based on SIC. Similar classifications with less industries can be found on Kenneth R. French's website. Bhojraj et al. (2003) argue that datastream improves its coverage dramatically in the mid-1990s, so it's a good practice to use the data 1995 onwards for global comparison (see Bhattacharya and Galpin, 2011; Morck et al., 2000). To classify a country as an emerging market or developed market, use the developed market index of Morgan Stanley Capital International (MSCI) (see Bhattacharya and Galpin, 2011, p. 744). Insider and institutional holding data come from Compact Disclosure (Loughran and Schultz, 2005, p. 350). For news events, it is typical to use the Dow Jones Archive. See Engelberg, Reed and Ringgenberg (2012, p. 264) and Tetlock (2010).

When we do microstructure studies, we need to be careful about some institutional background (Chung and Chuwonganant, 2004, p. 47). NASDAQ is a quote driven market before 1997, it becomes an order driven market due to the implementation of new Order Handling Rule (OHR) in 1997. But I guess it is incorrect to say NASDAQ had been transformed into an order driven market after 1997. In most literature, NASDAQ remains a quote driven market, with a lot of market makers. But the market makers on NASDAQ are relatively easy to enter and exit (Anand et al., 2011, p. 199). For Electronic Communication Networks (ECNs), see Anand et al. (2011) and Simaan et al. (2003).

Also on NASDAQ, brokers may route orders to a particular market maker in exchange for some payment from this market maker. The market maker will execute the order at the National Best Bid and Offer (NBBO) quote (Anand et al.; 2011, p. 200). This arrangement may discourage market makers to post informative quotes.

Underwriter Reputation: the prior market share of the gross proceeds of domestic SEOs and IPOs where they serve as lead underwriters for the calendar year prior to the event. (Altınkılıç and Hansen; 2003).

11.4.2 Information and risk

Information asymmetry

Information asymmetry. Moeller et al. (2007) argue that a stock's idiosyncratic risk can measure the asymmetric information. Idiosyncratic risk is the residual of the regression of stock return on the market return (Masulis and Kim, 2010).

Investor uncertainty: stock return volatility (Masulis and Kim, 2010; Autore and Kovacs, 2010).

Accuracy of signal

Nicolosi et al. (2009) use the method proposed by Hartzmark (1991) to proxy the accuracy of an investor's signal. See Nicolosi et al. (2009, pp. 322–324).

Price informativeness

In terms of market maker's contribution in price discovery, Anand et al. (2011) measure the proportion of time that a market maker provides best quotes, among other measures. Beside this measure, there are the weighted price contribution measure of Barclay and Warner (1993) and the information share measure of Hasbrouck (1995).

Measurement of price discovery: Hasbrouck's (1995) information shares measure (used by Huang (2002), Chakravarty et al. (2004), Kurov and Lasser (2004), Anand and Subrahmanyam (2008), Anand et al. (2011)), Barclay and

Warner's (1993) weighted price contribution measure (used by Huang (2002), Anand et al. (2011)), and Anand et al.'s (2011) proportion of best quotes measure.

Stock return risk

The risk that each trader takes: Coval and Shumway (2005, p. 10), which was first developed by Coval and Shumway (2001).

Besides betas and standard deviations of return, Lakonishok et al. (1994, p. 1543) also measure the fundamental risk: "To be fundamentally riskier, [risky] stocks must underperform [less risky] stocks with some frequency, and particularly in the states of the world when the marginal utility of wealth is high." So they "look at the frequency of superior (and inferior) performance..., as well as at their performance in bad states of the world, such as extreme down markets and economic recessions."

Risk of non-traded assets

See Driessen et al. (2012); Franzoni et al. (2012); Korteweg and Sorensen (2010). Among these, Driessen et al. (2012) explain the idea of the estimation.

Earnings surprise

"Standardized unexpected earnings (SUE), defined as the difference between a company's earnings in a given quarter and its earnings during the quarter a year before, scaled by the standard deviation of the company's earnings (Barberis et al., 1998, p. 311)."

11.4.3 Trading

Orders from individuals and institutions

The microstructure data typically do not contain the identifications of the investors behind the orders. To separate orders from individual and institutional investors, we have to make some inferences. There are two ways to do this. One is use the order size. The other is to use the identification of the brokerage houses, because brokerage houses often specialize in handling either individual or institutional investors. Obviously the second way is feasible only when the data contain brokerage house identifications, which is usually not the case. Griffin et al. (2003) mainly use the second way. Most literature uses the first way. Barclay and Warner (1993) define small, medium, and large orders by the 500 and 1000 shares as the thresholds. Griffin et al. (2003) check both ways and find the results reasonably agree with each other.

11.4.4 Firm characteristics

For other firm characteristics to control for, see Billett et al. (2011, p. 354).

Firm size

For all stocks in all exchanges, firms are classified as large if it larger than the median NYSE firms, and are classified as small if smaller than the median NYSE firm.

Capital structure adjustment

Debt issuance can be inferred from cash flow statement, or directly from SDC's issuance data. The former should be preferred because many of the issuances are debt rolling over or exercising of options. When we study capital structure adjustment, the adjustment must change the cash flow to a significant degree. See Hovakimian et al. (2001, Footnote 4, p. 4) for the definition.

11.4.5 Asset pricing related measures

Benchmark portfolios and their returns

See Cremers et al. (2010) for some discussions.

Fama & French 25 Portfolios

Fama and French (1993, p. 10) specify the construction of Fama & French 25 portfolios:

> In June of each year we sort NYSE stocks by size and (independently) by book-to-market equity. For the size sort, ME is measured at the end of June. For the book-to-market sort, ME is market equity at the end of December of $t-1$, and BE is book common equity for the fiscal year ending in calendar year $t-1$. We use NYSE breakpoints for ME and BE/ME to allocate NYSE, Amex, and (after 1972) NASDAQ stocks to five size quintiles and five book-to-market quintiles. We construct 25 portfolios from the intersections of the size and BE/ME quintiles and calculate value-weighted monthly returns on the portfolios from July of t to June of $t+1$. The excess returns on these 25 portfolios for July 1963 to December 1991 are the dependent variables for

stocks in the time-series regressions.

Book value = Book value of shareholder's equity + Balance sheet deferred taxes and investment tax credits (if available) - Book value of preferred stock (measure by the redemption, liquidation, or par value, depending on availability).

Risk free and market return

The risk free return is proxied by one month Treasury Bill rate of return.

Price ratios

The caption of Table I in Fama and French (1993, p. 11) specifies the constructions of earnings/price ratio and dividend yield:

> A portfolio's earnings/price ratio (E/P) for year t is the sum of equity income for the firms in the portfolio for the fiscal year ending in calendar year $t-1$, divided by the sum of their market equity in December of $t-1$. Equity income is income before extraordinary items, plus income statement deferred taxes, minus preferred dividends. A portfolio's dividend yield (D/P) for year t is the sum (across firms in the portfolio) of the dividends paid from July of $t-1$ to June of t, divided by the sum of market equity in June of $t-1$. We use the procedure described in Fama and French (1988) to estimate dividends.

Bibliography

Acharya, V., Engle, R. and Richardson, M. (2012). Capital shortfall: A new approach to ranking and regulating systemic risks, *American Economic Review* **102**(3): 59–64.

Acharya, V. V. and Johnson, T. C. (2010). More insiders, more insider trading: Evidence from private-equity buyouts, *Journal of Financial Economics* **98**(3): 500–523.

Acharya, V. V., Myers, S. C. and Rajan, R. G. (2011). The internal governance of firms, *The Journal of Finance* **66**(3): 689–720.

Acharya, V. V. and Pedersen, L. H. (2005). Asset pricing with liquidity risk, *Journal of Financial Economics* **77**(2): 375–410.

Acharya, V. V. and Viswanathan, S. (2011). Leverage, moral hazard, and liquidity, *The Journal of Finance* **66**(1): 99–138.

Adkins, R. and Paxson, D. (2011). Renewing assets with uncertain revenues and operating costs, *Journal of Financial and Quantitative Analysis* **46**(3): 785–813.

Admati, A. R. (1985). A noisy rational expectations equilibrium for multi-asset securities markets, *Econometrica* **53**(3): 629–657.

Admati, A. R. and Pfleiderer, P. (1988). A theory of intraday patterns: Volume and price variability, *Review of Financial Studies* (1): 3–40.

Afonso, G., Kovner, A. and Schoar, A. (2011). Stressed, not frozen: The Federal funds market in the financial crisis, *The Journal of Finance* **66**(4): 1109–1139.

Aggarwal, R. and Angel, J. J. (1999). The rise and fall of the amex emerging company marketplace, *Journal of Financial Economics* **52**(2): 257–289.

Aiello, S. and Chieffe, N. (1999). International index funds and the investment portfolio, *Financial Services Review* **8**(1): 27–35.

Aitken, M., Almeida, N., DeB. Harris, F. H. and McInish, T. H. (2007). Liquidity supply in electronic markets, *Journal of Financial Markets* **10**(2): 144–168.

Akhigbe, A., Newman, M. and Safieddine, A. (2006). Market expectations and the valuation effects of equity issuance, *Journal of Financial Research* **29**(2): 253–269.

Almazan, A., Brown, K. C., Carlson, M. and Chapman, D. A.(2004). Why constrain your mutual fund manager?, *Journal of Financial Economics* **73**(2): 289–321.

Altı, A. and Sulaeman, J. (2012). When do high stock returns trigger equity issues?, *Journal of Financial Economics* **103**(1): 61–87.

Altınkılıç, O., Balashov, V. S. and Hansen, R. S. (2013). Are analysts' forecasts informative to the general public?, *Management Science* **59**(11): 2550–2565.

Altınkılıç, O. and Hansen, R. S. (2003). Discounting and underpricing in seasoned equity offers, *Journal of Financial Economics* **69**(2): 285–323.

Amihud, Y. (2002). Illiquidity and stock returns: cross-section and time-series effects, *Journal of Financial Markets* **5**(1): 31–56.

Amihud, Y. and Goyenko, R. (2013). Mutual fund's R2 as predictor of performance, *Review of Financial Studies* **26**(3): 667 –694.

Amihud, Y. and Mendelson, H. (1980). Dealership market : Market-making with inventory, *Journal of Financial Economics* **8**(1): 31–53.

Amihud, Y. and Mendelson, H. (1986a). Asset pricing and the bid-ask spread, *Journal of Financial Economics* **17**(2): 223–249.

Amihud, Y. and Mendelson, H. (1986b). Liquidity and stock returns, *Financial Analysts Journal* **42**(3): 43–48.

Anand, A., Gatchev, V. A., Madureira, L., Pirinsky, C. A. and Underwood, S. (2011). Geographic proximity and price discovery: *Evidence from NASDAQ, Journal of Financial Markets* **14**(2): 193–226.

Anand, A. and Subrahmanyam, A. (2008). Information and the intermediary: Are market intermediaries informed traders in electronic markets?, *Journal of Financial and Quantitative Analysis* **43**(1): 1–28.

Anderson, C. W. and Garcia-Feijóo, L. (2006). Empirical evidence on capital investment, growth options, and security returns, *The Journal of Finance* **61**(1): 171–194.

Asparouhova, E., Hertzel, M. and Lemmon, M. (2009). Inference from streaks in random outcomes: Experimental evidence on beliefs in regime shifting and the law of small numbers, *Management Science* **55**(11): 1766 –1782.

Asquith, P. and Mullins, D. W. (1986). Equity issues and offering dilution, *Journal of Financial Economics* **15**(12): 61–89.

Asquith, P., Pathak, P. A. and Ritter, J. R. (2005). Short interest, institutional ownership, and stock returns, *Journal of Financial Economics* **78**(2): 243–276.

Atanasov, V., Ivanov, V. and Litvak, K. (2012). Does reputation limit opportunistic behavior in the VC industry? Evidence from litigation against VCs, *The Journal of Finance* **67**(6): 2215–2246.

Autore, D. M. and Kovacs, T. (2010). Equity issues and temporal variation in information asymmetry, *Journal of Banking & Finance* **34**(1): 12–23.

Avramov, D. and Zhou, G. (2010). Bayesian portfolio analysis, *Annual Review of Financial Economics* **2**(1): 25–47.

Back, K. and Baruch, S. (2007). Working orders in limit order markets and floor exchanges, *The Journal of Finance* **62**(4): 1589–1621.

Back, K., Cao, C. H. and Willard, G. A. (2000). Imperfect competition among informed traders, *The Journal of Finance* **55**(5): 2117–2155.

Badrinath, S. G. and Wahal, S. (2002). Momentum trading by institutions, *The Journal of Finance* **57**(6): 2449–2478.

Bagehot, W. (1971). The only game in town, *Financial Analysts Journal* **27**: 12– 14.

Baker, M., Pan, X. and Wurgler, J. (2012). The effect of reference point prices on mergers and acquisitions, *Journal of Financial Economics* **106**(1): 49–71.

Baker, M., Stein, J. C. and Wurgler, J. (2003). When does the market matter? Stock prices and the investment of equity-dependent firms, *The Quarterly Journal of Economics* **118**(3): 969–1005.

Baker, M. and Wurgler, J. (2002). Market timing and capital structure, *The Journal of Finance* **57**(1): 1–32.

Baks, K. P., Metrick, A. and Wachter, J. (2001). Should investors avoid all actively managed mutual funds? A study in Bayesian performance evaluation, *The Journal of Finance* **56**(1): 45–85.

Bamber, L. S., Barron, O. E. and Stober, T. L. (1999). Differential interpretations and trading volume, *Journal of Financial and Quantitative Analysis* **34**(3): 369–386.

Banerjee, A. V. (1992). A simple model of herd behavior, *The Quarterly Journal of Economics* **107**(3): 797–817.

Bao, J. and Edmans, A. (2011). Do investment banks matter for M&A returns?, *Review of Financial Studies* **24**(7): 2286 –2315.

Barber, B. M. and Odean, T. (2001). Boys will be boys: Gender, overconfidence, and common stock investment, *The Quarterly Journal of Economics* **116**(1): 261 –292.

Barber, B. M. and Odean, T. (2008). All that glitters: The effect of attention and news on the buying behavior of individual and institutional investors, *Review of Financial Studies* **21**(2): 785–818.

Barber, B. M., Odean, T. and Zheng, L. (2005). Out of sight, out of mind: the effects of expenses on mutual fund flows, *The Journal of Business* **78**(6): 2095–

2120.

Barber, B. M., Odean, T. and Zhu, N. (2006). Systematic noise, SSRN eLibrary .

Barber, B. M., Odean, T. and Zhu, N. (2009). Systematic noise, *Journal of Financial Markets* **12**(4): 547–569.

Barberis, N. and Huang, M. (2008). Stocks as lotteries: The implications of probability weighting for security prices, *American Economic Review* **98**(5): 2066–2100.

Barberis, N. and Shleifer, A. (2003). *Style investing, Journal of Financial Economics* **68**(2): 161–199.

Barberis, N., Shleifer, A. and Vishny, R. (1998). A model of investor sentiment, *Journal of Financial Economics* **49**(3): 307–343.

Barberis, N. and Xiong, W. (2012). Realization utility, *Journal of Financial Economics* **104**(2): 251–271.

Barclay, M. J., Christie, W. G., Harris, J. H., Kandel, E. and Schultz, P. H. (1999). Effects of market reform on the trading costs and depths of NASDAQ stocks, *The Journal of Finance* **54**(1): 1–34.

Barclay, M. J. and Holderness, C. G. (1992). The law and large-block trades, *Journal of Law and Economics* **35**(2): 265–294.

Barclay, M. J. and Warner, J. B. (1993). Stealth trading and volatility : Which trades move prices?, *Journal of Financial Economics* **34**(3): 281–305.

Barsky, R. B., Juster, F. T., Kimball, M. S. and Shapiro, M. D. (1997). Preference parameters and behavioral heterogeneity: An experimental approach in the health and retirement study, *The Quarterly Journal of Economics* **112**(2): 537 –579.

Bartling, B. and Park, A. (2010). How syndicate short sales affect the informational efficiency of IPO prices and underpricing, *Journal of Financial and Quantitative Analysis* **45**(2): 441–471.

Bartram, S. M., Brown, G. and Stulz, R. M. (2012). Why are U.S. stocks more volatile?, *The Journal of Finance* **67**(4): 1329–1370.

Baruch, S. (2002). Insider trading and risk aversion, *Journal of Financial Markets* **5**(4): 451–464.

Basak, S. (2005). Asset pricing with heterogeneous beliefs, *Journal of Banking & Finance* **29**(11): 2849–2881.

Basak, S., Pavlova, A. and Shapiro, A. (2007). Optimal asset allocation and risk shifting in money management, *Review of Financial Studies* **20**(5): 1583–1621.

Battalio, R. H., Hatch, B. and Jennings, R. (1997). SOES trading and market volatility, *Journal of Financial and Quantitative Analysis* **32**(2): 225–238.

Bayless, M. and Chaplinsky, S. (1996). Is there a window of opportunity for seasoned equity issuance?, *The Journal of Finance* **51**(1): 253–278.

Bekaert, G., Harvey, C. R. and Lundblad, C. (2007). Liquidity and expected returns: Lessons from emerging markets, *Review of Financial Studies* **20**(6): 1783 –1831.

Ben-David, I., Franzoni, F. and Moussawi, R. (2012). Hedge fund stock trading in the financial crisis of 2007-2009, *Review of Financial Studies* **25**(1): 1 –54.

Bennett, J. A., Sias, R. W. and Starks, L. T. (2003). Greener pastures and the impact of dynamic institutional preferences, *Review of Financial Studies* **16**(4): 1203–1238.

Benninga, S., Helmantel, M. and Sarig, O. (2005). The timing of initial public offerings, *Journal of Financial Economics* **75**(1): 115–132.

Benveniste, L. M. and Spindt, P. A. (1989). How investment bankers determine the offer price and allocation of new issues, *Journal of Financial Economics* **24**(2): 343–361.

Bergstresser, D., Chalmers, J. M. R. and Tufano, P. (2009). Assessing the costs and benefits of brokers in the mutual fund industry, *Review of Financial Studies* **22**(10): 4129 –4156.

Berk, J. B. and Green, R. C. (2004). Mutual fund flows and performance in rational markets, *Journal of Political Economy* **112**(6): 1269–1295.

Berk, J. B. and Stanton, R. (2007). Managerial ability, compensation, and the closed-end fund discount, *The Journal of Finance* **62**(2): 529–556.

Bernard, V. L. and Thomas, J. K. (1990). Evidence that stock prices do not fully reflect the implications of current earnings for future earnings, *Journal of Accounting and Economics* **13**(4): 305–340.

Bernhardt, D. and Hughson, E. (2002). Intraday trade in dealership markets, *European Economic Review* **46**(9): 1697–1732.

Bettis, J. C., Coles, J. L. and Lemmon, M. L. (2000). Corporate policies restricting trading by insiders, *Journal of Financial Economics* **57**(2): 191–220.

Bhattacharya, U. and Galpin, N. (2011). The global rise of the value-weighted portfolio, *Journal of Financial and Quantitative Analysis* **46**(3): 737–756.

Bhojraj, S., Lee, C. M. C. and Oler, D. K. (2003). What's my line? A comparison of industry classification schemes for capital market research, *Journal of Accounting Research* **41**(5): 745–774.

Biais, B. (1993). Price formation and equilibrium liquidity in fragmented and centralized markets, *The Journal of Finance* **48**(1): 157–185.

Biais, B., Hillion, P. and Spatt, C. (1995). An empirical analysis of the limit order book and the order flow in the Paris Bourse, *The Journal of Finance* **50**(5): 1655–1689.

Bikhchandani, S., Hirshleifer, D. and Welch, I. (1992). A theory of fads, fashion, custom, and cultural change as informational cascades, *Journal of Political Economy* **100**(5): 992–1026.

Billett, M. T., Flannery, M. J. and Garfinkel, J. A. (2011). Frequent issuers' influence on long-run post-issuance returns, *Journal of Financial Economics* **99**(2): 349–364.

Black, F. (1986). Noise, *The Journal of Finance* **41**(3): 529–543.

Blanchard, O., Rhee, C. and Summers, L. (1993). The stock market, profit, and investment, *The Quarterly Journal of Economics* **108**(1): 115–136.

Bloomfield, R., O'Hara, M. and Saar, G. (2005). The "make or take" decision in an electronic market: Evidence on the evolution of liquidity, *Journal of Financial Economics* **75**(1): 165–199.

Bloomfield, R., O'Hara, M. and Saar, G. (2009). How noise trading affects markets: An experimental analysis, *Review of Financial Studies* **22**(6): 2275 –2302.

Blume, L. E. and Easley, D. (1982). Learning to be rational, *Journal of Economic Theory* **26**(2): 340–351.

Blume, L. and Easley, D. (2006). If you're so smart, why aren't you rich? Belief selection in complete and incomplete markets, *Econometrica* **74**(4): 929–966.

Boehmer, E., Jones, C. M. and Zhang, X. (2008). Which shorts are informed?, *The Journal of Finance* **63**(2): 491–527.

Boehmer, E. and Wu, J. J. (2013). Short selling and the price discovery process, *Review of Financial Studies* **26**(2): 287 –322.

Bogle, J. C. (2005). The mutual fund industry 60 years later: for better or worse?, *Financial Analysts Journal* **61**(1): 15–24.

Boldin, M. and Cici, G. (2010). The index fund rationality paradox, *Journal of Banking & Finance* **34**(1): 33–43.

Bond, P., Goldstein, I. and Prescott, E. S. (2010). Market-based corrective actions, *Review of Financial Studies* **23**(2): 781 –820.

Bongaerts, D., De Jong, F. and Driessen, J. (2011). Derivative pricing with liquidity risk: Theory and evidence from the credit default swap market, *The Journal of Finance* **66**(1): 203–240.

Bouchaud, J.-P., Mézard, M. and Potters, M. (2002). Statistical properties of stock order books: empirical results and models, *Quantitative Finance* **2**(4): 251–256.

Boulatov, A., Hendershott, T. and Livdan, D. (2013). Informed trading and portfolio returns, *The Review of Economic Studies* **80**(1): 35 –72.

Bradley, M., Brav, A., Goldstein, I. and Jiang, W. (2010). Activist arbitrage: A study of open-ending attempts of closed-end funds, *Journal of Financial Economics* **95**(1): 1–19.

Brav, A. and Heaton, J. B. (2002). Competing theories of financial anomalies, *Review of Financial Studies* **15**(2): 575 –606.

Bray, M. and Savin, N. E. (1986). Rational expectations equilibria, learning, and model specification, *Econometrica* **54**(5): 1129–1160.

Brennan, M. J. and Cao, H. H. (1997). International portfolio investment flows, *The Journal of Finance* **52**(5): 1851–1880.

Brennan, M. J., Chordia, T. and Subrahmanyam, A. (1998). Alternative factor specifications, security characteristics, and the cross-section of expected stock returns, *Journal of Financial Economics* **49**(3): 345–373.

Brennan, M. J., Chordia, T., Subrahmanyam, A. and Tong, Q. (2012). Sellorder liquidity and the cross-section of expected stock returns, *Journal of Financial Economics* **105**(3): 523–541.

Brennan, M. J. and Subrahmanyam, A. (1996). Market microstructure and asset pricing: On the compensation for illiquidity in stock returns, *Journal of Financial Economics* **41**(3): 441–464.

Bris, A. (2005). Do insider trading laws work?, *European Financial Management* **11**(3): 267–312.

Brockman, P. and Chung, D. Y. (1999). An analysis of depth behavior in an electronic, order-driven environment, *Journal of Banking & Finance* **23**(12): 1861–1886.

Brockman, P. and Chung, D. Y. (2002). The impact of informed trading on corporate liquidity, *Journal of Multinational Financial Management* **12**(3): 239–259.

Brockman, P., Chung, D. Y. and Pérignon, C. (2009). Commonality in liquidity: A global perspective, *Journal of Financial and Quantitative Analysis* **44**(4): 851–882.

Brown, J. (2011). Quitters never win: The (adverse) incentive effects of competing with superstars, *Journal of Political Economy* **119**(5): 982–1013.

Brown, J. R., Ivković, Z., Smith, P. A. and Weisbenner, S. (2008). Neighbors matter: Causal community effects and stock market participation, *The Journal of Finance* **63**(3): 1509–1531.

Brown, K. C., Harlow, W. V. and Starks, L. T. (1996). Of tournaments and temptations: An analysis of managerial incentives in the mutual fund industry, *The Journal of Finance* **51**(1): 85–110.

Brown, S. J. and Goetzmann, W. N. (1995). Performance persistence, *The Journal of Finance* **50**(2): 679–698.

Brown, S. J. and Goetzmann, W. N. (1997). Mutual fund styles, *Journal of Financial Economics* **43**(3): 373–399.

Brown, S. J. and Goetzmann, W. N. (2003). Hedge funds with style, *Journal of Portfolio Management* **29**(2): 101–112.

Brunnermeier, M. K. and Pedersen, L. H. (2009). Market liquidity and funding liquidity, *Review of Financial Studies* **22**(6): 2201 –2238.

Burgess, R. C. and O'Dell, B. T. (1978). An empirical examination of index efficiency: Implications for index funds, *Journal of Financial and Quantitative Analysis* **13**(1): 93–100.

Busse, J. A. (2001). Another look at mutual fund tournaments, *Journal of Financial and Quantitative Analysis* **36**(1): 53–73.

Butler, A. W. and Wan, H. (2010). Stock market liquidity and the long-run stock performance of debt issuers, *Review of Financial Studies* **23**(11): 3966 –3995.

Byoun, S. (2008). How and when do firms adjust their capital structures toward targets?, *The Journal of Finance* **63**(6): 3069–3096.

Calvet, L. E., Campbell, J. Y. and Sodini, P. (2009). Fight or flight? Portfolio rebalancing by individual investors, *The Quarterly Journal of Economics* **124**(1): 301 –348.

Camerer, C. F. and Hogarth, R. M. (1999). The effects of financial incentives in experiments: A review and capital-labor-production framework, *Journal of Risk and Uncertainty* 19(1): 7–42.

Cao, C., Chang, E. C. and Wang, Y. (2008). An empirical analysis of the dynamic relationship between mutual fund flow and market return volatility, *Journal of Banking & Finance* **32**(10): 2111–2123.

Cao, C., Field, L. C. and Gordon, H. (2004). Does insider trading impair market liquidity? Evidence from IPO lockup expirations, *Journal of Financial and Quantitative Analysis* **39**(1): 25–46.

Cao, C., Ghysels, E. and Hatheway, F. (2000). Price discovery without trading: Evidence from the Nasdaq preopening, *The Journal of Finance* **55**(3): 1339–1365.

Capon, N., Fitzsimons, G. J. and Prince, R. A. (1996). An individual level analysis of the mutual fund investment decision, *Journal of Financial Services Research* **10**(1): 59–82.

Carhart, M. M. (1997). On persistence in mutual fund performance, *The Journal of Finance* **52**(1): 57–82.

Carlson, M., Fisher, A. and Giammarino, R. (2006). Corporate investment and asset price dynamics: Implications for SEO event studies and long-run performance, *The Journal of Finance* **61**(3): 1009–1034.

Carpenter, J.N.(2000). Does option compensation increase managerial risk appetite?, *The Journal of Finance* **55**(5): 2311–2331.

Caskey, J. A. (2009). Information in equity markets with ambiguity-averse investors, *Review of Financial Studies* **22**(9): 3595 –3627.

Chakravarty, S. (2001). Stealth-trading: Which traders' trades move stock prices?, *Journal of Financial Economics* **61**(2): 289–307.

Chakravarty, S., Gulen, H. and Mayhew, S. (2004). Informed trading in stock and option markets, *The Journal of Finance* **59**(3): 1235–1258.

Chakravarty, S. and Holden, C. W. (1995). An integrated model of market and limit orders, *Journal of Financial Intermediation* **4**(3): 213–241.

Chan, L. K. C., Chen, H.-L. and Lakonishok, J. (2002). On mutual fund investment styles, *Review of Financial Studies* **15**(5): 1407–1437.

Chandra, U. and Nayar, N. N. (2008). The information content of private debt placements, *Journal of Business Finance & Accounting* **35**(910): 1164–1195.

Charness, G. and Levin, D. (2005). When optimal choices feel wrong: A laboratory study of Bayesian updating, complexity, and affect, *American Economic Review* **95**(4): 1300–1309.

Chatterjee, S., John, K. and Yan, A. (2012). Takeovers and divergence of investor opinion, *Review of Financial Studies* **25**(1): 227 –277.

Chava, S. and Roberts, M. R. (2008). How does financing impact investment? The role of debt covenants, *The Journal of Finance* **63**(5): 2085–2121.

Chemmanur, T. J. and Fulghieri, P. (1999). A theory of the going-public decision, *Review of Financial Studies* **12**(2): 249–279.

Chemmanur, T. J., He, S. and Hu, G. (2009). The role of institutional investors in seasoned equity offerings, *Journal of Financial Economics* **94**(3): 384–411.

Chemmanur, T. J. and Jiao, Y. (2011). Institutional trading, information production, and the SEO discount: A model of seasoned equity offerings, *Journal of Economics & Management Strategy* **20**(1): 299–338.

Chen, H.-L. and Pennacchi, G. G. (2009). Does prior performance affect a mutual fund's choice of risk? Theory and further empirical evidence, *Journal of Financial and Quantitative Analysis* **44**(4): 745–775.

Chen, J., Hong, H., Huang, M. and Kubik, J. D. (2004). Does fund size erode mutual fund performance? The role of liquidity and organization, *American Economic Review* **94**(5): 1276–1302.

Chen, J., Hong, H. and Stein, J. C. (2001). Forecasting crashes: trading volume, past returns, and conditional skewness in stock prices, *Journal of Financial Economics* **61**(3): 345–381.

Chen, J., Hong, H. and Stein, J. C. (2002). Breadth of ownership and stock returns, *Journal of Financial Economics* **66**(23): 171–205.

Chen, Q., Goldstein, I. and Jiang, W. (2010). Payoff complementarities and financial fragility: Evidence from mutual fund outflows, *Journal of Financial Economics* **97**(2): 239–262.

Cherkes, M., Sagi, J. and Stanton, R. (2009). A liquidity-based theory of closedend funds, *Review of Financial Studies* **22**(1): 257 –297.

Chevalier, J. and Ellison, G. (1997). Risk taking by mutual funds as a response to incentives, *Journal of Political Economy* **105**(6): 1167–1200.

Chevalier, J. and Ellison, G. (1999). Are some mutual fund managers better than others? Cross-sectional patterns in behavior and performance, *The Journal of Finance* **54**(3): 875–899.

Choe, H., Kho, B.-C. and Stulz, R. M. (1999). Do foreign investors destabilize stock markets? The Korean experience in 1997, *Journal of Financial Economics* **54**(2): 227–264.

Choe, H., Masulis, R. W. and Nanda, V. (1993). Common stock offerings across the business cycle: Theory and evidence, *Journal of Empirical Finance* **1**(1): 3–31.

Choi, J. J., Laibson, D. and Madrian, B. C. (2010). Why does the law of one price fail? An experiment on index mutual funds, *Review of Financial Studies* **23**(4): 1405 –1432.

Choi, J. J., Laibson, D., Madrian, B. C. and Metrick, A. (2009). Reinforcement learning and savings behavior, *The Journal of Finance* **64**(6): 2515–2534.

Choi, N. and Sias, R. W. (2009). Institutional industry herding, *Journal of*

Financial Economics **94**(3): 469–491.

Chopra, N., Lakonishok, J. and Ritter, J. R. (1992). Measuring abnormal performance: Do stocks overreact?, *Journal of Financial Economics* **31**(2): 235–268.

Chordia, T. (1996). The structure of mutual fund charges, *Journal of Financial Economics* **41**(1): 3–39.

Chordia, T., Roll, R. and Subrahmanyam, A. (2000). Commonality in liquidity, *Journal of Financial Economics* **56**(1): 3–28.

Chordia, T., Roll, R. and Subrahmanyam, A. (2001). Market liquidity and trading activity, *The Journal of Finance* **56**(2): 501–530.

Chordia, T., Sarkar, A. and Subrahmanyam, A. (2005). An empirical analysis of stock and bond market liquidity, *Review of Financial Studies* **18**(1): 85–129.

Chordia, T., Subrahmanyam, A. and Anshuman, V. R. (2001). Trading activity and expected stock returns, *Journal of Financial Economics* **59**(1): 3–32.

Christensen, P. O., Rosa, L. E. D. L. and Feltham, G. A. (2010). Information and the cost of capital: An ex ante perspective, *Accounting review* **85**(3): 817–848.

Christie, W. G. and Huang, R. D. (1994). Market structures and liquidity: A transactions data study of exchange listings, *Journal of Financial Intermediation* **3**(3): 300–326.

Christie, W. G. and Schultz, P. H. (1994). Why do NASDAQ market makers avoid odd-eighth quotes?, *The Journal of Finance* **49**(5): 1813–1840.

Christoffersen, S. E. K. and Musto, D. K. (2002). Demand curves and the pricing of money management, *Review of Financial Studies* **15**(5): 1499–1524.

Chung, K. H. and Chuwonganant, C. (2004). Tick size, order handling rules, and trading costs, *Financial Management* **33**(1): 47–62.

Chung, K. H., Chuwonganant, C. and Jiang, J. (2008). The dynamics of quote adjustments, *Journal of Banking & Finance* **32**(11): 2390–2400.

Chung, K. H., Elder, J. and Kim, J.-C. (2010). Corporate governance and liquidity, *Journal of Financial and Quantitative Analysis* **45**(2): 265–291.

Chung, K. H., van Ness, B. F. and van Ness, R. A. (2001). Can the treatment of limit orders reconcile the differences in trading costs between NYSE and Nasdaq issues?, *Journal of Financial and Quantitative Analysis* **36**(2): 267– 286.

Cochrane, J. H. (2011). Presidential address: Discount rates, *The Journal of Finance* **66**(4): 1047–1108.

Cohen, L., Frazzini, A. and Malloy, C. (2008). The small world of investing: board connections and mutual fund returns, *Journal of Political Economy* **116**(5): 951–979.

Cohen, R. B., Coval, J. D. and Pástor, Ł. (2005). Judging fund managers by the company they keep, *The Journal of Finance*(3): 1057–1096.

Cohen, R. B., Gompers, P. A. and Vuolteenaho, T. (2002). Who underreacts to cash-flow news? Evidence from trading between individuals and institutions,

Journal of Financial Economics **66**(23): 409–462.

Colla, P. and Mele, A. (2010). Information linkages and correlated trading, *Review of Financial Studies* **23**(1): 203 –246.

Comerton-Forde, C., Hendershott, T., Jones, C. M., Moulton, P. C. and Seasholes, M. S. (2010). Time variation in liquidity: The role of marketmaker inventories and revenues, *The Journal of Finance* **65**(1): 295–331.

Conrad, J., Kaul, G. and Nimalendran, M. (1991). Components of short-horizon individual security returns, *Journal of Financial Economics* **29**(2): 365–384.

Cooper, I. and Kaplanis, E. (1994). Home bias in equity portfolios, inflation hedging, and international capital market equilibrium, *Review of Financial Studies* **7**(1): 45 –60.

Corwin, S. A. (2003). The determinants of underpricing for seasoned equity offers, *The Journal of Finance* **58**(5): 2249–2279.

Corwin, S. A. and Lipson, M. L. (2011). Order characteristics and the sources of commonality in prices and liquidity, *Journal of Financial Markets* **14**(1): 47–81.

Coughenour, J. F. and Saad, M. M. (2004). Common market makers and commonality in liquidity, *Journal of Financial Economics* **73**(1): 37–69.

Coursey, D. L., Hovis, J. L. and Schulze, W. D. (1987). The disparity between willingness to accept and willingness to pay measures of value, *The Quarterly Journal of Economics* **102**(3): 679 –690.

Coval, J. D., Hirshleifer, D. A. and Shumway, T. (2005). Can individual investors beat the market?, SSRN eLibrary .

Coval, J. D. and Shumway, T. (2001). Is sound just noise?, *The Journal of Finance* **56**(5): 1887–1910.

Coval, J. D. and Shumway, T. (2005). Do behavioral biases affect prices?, *The Journal of Finance* **60**(1): 1–34.

Cremers, K. J. M. and Petajisto, A. (2009). How active is your fund manager? A new measure that predicts performance, *Review of Financial Studies* **22**(9): 3329 –3365.

Cremers, M., Petajisto, A. and Zitzewitz, E. (2010). Should benchmark indices have alpha? Revisiting performance evaluation, SSRN eLibrary .

Cronqvist, H., Makhija, A. K. and Yonker, S. E. (2012). Behavioral consistency in corporate finance: CEO personal and corporate leverage, *Journal of Financial Economics* **103**(1): 20–40.

Cronqvist, H. and Nilsson, M. (2005). The choice between rights offerings and private equity placements, *Journal of Financial Economics* **78**(2): 375–407.

Cuoco, D. and Kaniel, R. (2011). Equilibrium prices in the presence of delegated portfolio management, *Journal of Financial Economics* **101**(2): 264–296.

Cutler, D. M., Poterba, J. M. and Summers, L. H. (1991). Speculative dynamics, *The Review of Economic Studies* **58**(3): 529 –546.

Da, Z. and Warachka, M. (2011). The disparity between long-term and short-term forecasted earnings growth, *Journal of Financial Economics* **100**(2): 424–442.

Dang, T. V., Gorton, G. and Holmström, B. (2010). Financial crises and the optimality of debt for liquidity, Working Paper .

Dangl, T., Wu, Y. and Zechner, J. (2008). Market discipline and internal governance in the mutual fund industry, *Review of Financial Studies* **21**(5): 2307– 2343.

Daniel, K. D., Hirshleifer, D. and Subrahmanyam, A. (2001). Overconfidence, arbitrage, and equilibrium asset pricing, *The Journal of Finance* **56**(3): 921– 965.

Daniel, K., Hirshleifer, D. and Subrahmanyam, A. (1998). Investor psychology and security market under- and overreactions, *The Journal of Finance* **53**(6): 1839–1885.

Daniel, K., Hirshleifer, D. and Teoh, S. H. (2002). Investor psychology in capital markets: evidence and policy implications, *Journal of Monetary Economics* **49**(1): 139–209.

Daniel, K. and Titman, S. (1999). Market efficiency in an irrational world, *Financial Analysts Journal* **55**(6): 28–40.

Danielsen, B. R. and Sorescu, S. M. (2001). Why do option introductions depress stock prices? A study of diminishing short sale constraints, *Journal of Financial and Quantitative Analysis* **36**(4): 451–484.

Das, S. R. and Sundaram, R. K. (2002). Fee speech: Signaling, risk-sharing, and the impact of fee structures on investor welfare, *Review of Financial Studies* **15**(5): 1465–1497.

Dasgupta, A., Prat, A. and Verardo, M. (2011). The price impact of institutional herding, *Review of Financial Studies* **24**(3): 892 –925.

Dass, N., Massa, M. and Patgiri, R. (2008). Mutual funds and bubbles: the surprising role of contractual incentives, *Review of Financial Studies* **21**(1): 51–99.

Datar, V. T., Y. Naik, N. and Radcliffe, R. (1998). Liquidity and stock returns: An alternative test, *Journal of Financial Markets* **1**(2): 203–219.

De Bondt, W. F. M. and Thaler, R. H. (1985). Does the stock market overreact?, *The Journal of Finance* **40**(3): 793–805.

De Bondt, W. F. M. and Thaler, R. H. (1987). Further evidence on investor overreaction and stock market seasonality, *The Journal of Finance* **42**(3): 557–581.

de Jong, F., Nijman, T. and Röell, A. (1996). Price effects of trading and components of the bid-ask spread on the Paris Bourse, *Journal of Empirical Finance* **3**(2): 193–213.

De Long, J. B., Shleifer, A., Summers, L. H. and Waldmann, R. J. (1990a). Noise trader risk in financial markets, *Journal of Political Economy* **98**(4): 703–

738.

De Long, J. B., Shleifer, A., Summers, L. H. and Waldmann, R. J. (1990b). Positive feedback investment strategies and destabilizing rational speculation, *The Journal of Finance* **45**(2): 379–395.

DeAngelo, H., DeAngelo, L. and Stulz, R. M. (2010). Seasoned equity offerings, market timing, and the corporate lifecycle, *Journal of Financial Economics* **95**(3): 275–295.

Del Guercio, D. and Tkac, P. A. (2002). The determinants of the flow of funds of managed portfolios: mutual funds vs. pension funds, *Journal of Financial and Quantitative Analysis* **37**(4): 523–557.

Deli, D. N. (2002). Mutual fund advisory contracts: An empirical investigation, *The Journal of Finance* **57**(1): 109–133.

DeMarzo, P. M., Fishman, M. J. and Hagerty, K. M. (1998). The optimal enforcement of insider trading regulations, *Journal of Political Economy* **106**(3): 602–632.

Demarzo, P. M., Ron, K. and Kremer, I. (2004). Diversification as a public good: Community effects in portfolio choice, *The Journal of Finance* **59**(4): 1677– 1715.

Denis, D. J. and Mihov, V. T. (2003). The choice among bank debt, nonbank private debt, and public debt: evidence from new corporate borrowings, *Journal of Financial Economics* **70**(1): 3–28.

Dermine, J. and Röller, L.-H. (1992). Economies of scale and scope in French mutual funds, *Journal of Financial Intermediation* **2**(1): 83–93.

Devenow, A. and Welch, I. (1996). Rational herding in financial economics, *European Economic Review* **40**(35): 603–615.

Dhar, R. and Zhu, N. (2006). Up close and personal: Investor sophistication and the disposition effect, *Management Science* **52**(5): 726–740.

Diether, K. B., Malloy, C. J. and Scherbina, A. (2002). Differences of opinion and the cross section of stock returns, *The Journal of Finance* **57**(5): 2113– 2141.

Ding, B., Getmansky, M., Liang, B. and Wermers, R. R. (2011). Share restrictions and investor flows in the hedge fund industry, SSRN eLibrary .

Domowitz, I., Hansch, O. and Wang, X. (2005). Liquidity commonality and return co-movement, *Journal of Financial Markets* **8**(4): 351–376.

Dorn, D., Huberman, G. and Sengmueller, P. (2008). Correlated trading and returns, *The Journal of Finance* **63**(2): 885–920.

Driessen, J., Lin, T.-C. and Phalippou, L. (2012). A new method to estimate risk and return of nontraded assets from cash flows: The case of private equity funds, *Journal of Financial and Quantitative Analysis* **47**(3): 511–535.

Duarte, J. and Young, L. (2009). Why is PIN priced?, *Journal of Financial Economics* **91**(2): 119–138.

Dubofsky, D. A. (2010). Mutual fund portfolio trading and investor flow, *Journal of Banking & Finance* **34**(4): 802–812.

Duffie, D., Malamud, S. and Manso, G. (2010). The relative contributions of private information sharing and public information releases to information aggregation, *Journal of Economic Theory* **145**(4): 1574–1601.

Dybvig, P. H., Farnsworth, H. K. and Carpenter, J. N. (2010). Portfolio performance and agency, *Review of Financial Studies* **23**(1): 1–23.

Easley, D., Engle, R. F., O'Hara, M. and Wu, L. (2008). Time-varying arrival rates of informed and uninformed trades, *Journal of Financial Econometrics* **6**(2): 171 –207.

Easley, D., Hvidkjaer, S. and O'Hara, M. (2002). Is information risk a determinant of asset returns?, *The Journal of Finance* **57**(5): 2185–2221.

Easley, D., López de Prado, M. M. and O'Hara, M. (2012). Flow toxicity and liquidity in a high-frequency world, *Review of Financial Studies* **25**(5): 1457 –1493.

Easley, D. and O'Hara, M. (1987). Price, trade size, and information in securities markets, *Journal of Financial Economics* **19**(1): 69–90.

Easley, D. and O'Hara, M. (2004). Information and the cost of capital, *The Journal of Finance* **59**(4): 1553–1583.

Eckbo, B. E. and Norli, Ø. (2005). Liquidity risk, leverage and long-run IPO returns, *Journal of Corporate Finance* **11**(12): 1–35.

Economides, N. and Schwartz, R. A. (1995). Equity trading practices and market structure: Assessing asset managers' demand for immediacy, Financial Markets, *Institutions & Instruments* **4**(4): 1–46.

Edelen, R. M. (1999). Investor flows and the assessed performance of open-end mutual funds, *Journal of Financial Economics* **53**(3): 439–466.

Edgerton, J. (2012). Agency problems in public firms: Evidence from corporate jets in leveraged buyouts, *The Journal of Finance* **67**(6): 2187–2213.

Edmans, A., Goldstein, I. and Jiang, W. (2012). The real effects of financial markets: The impact of prices on takeovers, *The Journal of Finance* **67**(3): 933–971.

El Ghoul, S., Guedhami, O., Ni, Y., Pittman, J. and Saadi, S. (2013). Does information asymmetry matter to equity pricing? Evidence from firms' geographic location, *Contemporary Accounting Research* **30**(1): 140–181.

Ellis, K., Michaely, R. and O'Hara, M. (2000). When the underwriter is the market maker: An examination of trading in the IPO aftermarket, *The Journal of Finance* **55**(3): 1039–1074.

Ellul, A., Holden, C. W., Jain, P. and Jennings, R. (2007). Order dynamics: Recent evidence from the NYSE, *Journal of Empirical Finance* **14**(5): 636– 661.

Elton, E. J., Gruber, M. J. and Blake, C. R. (1996a). The persistence of riskadjusted mutual fund performance, *The Journal of Business* **69**(2): 133–157.

Elton, E. J., Gruber, M. J. and Blake, C. R. (1996b). Survivor bias and mutual fund performance, *Review of Financial Studies* **9**(4): 1097–1120.

Elton, E. J., Gruber, M. J. and Blake, C. R. (2003). Incentive fees and mutual funds, *The Journal of Finance* **58**(2): 779–804.

Elton, E. J., Gruber, M. J. and Busse, J. A. (2004). Are investors rational? choices among index funds, *The Journal of Finance* **59**(1): 261–288.

Elton, E. J., Gruber, M. J., Das, S. and Hlavka, M. (1993). Efficiency with costly information: A reinterpretation of evidence from managed portfolios, *Review of Financial Studies* **6**(1): 1–22.

Engelberg, J. E., Reed, A. V. and Ringgenberg, M. C. (2012). How are shorts informed?: Short sellers, news, and information processing, *Journal of Financial Economics* **105**(2): 260–278.

Engelberg, J., Gao, P. and Parsons, C. A. (2012). Friends with money, *Journal of Financial Economics* **103**(1): 169–188.

Epstein, L. G. and Zin, S. E. (1989). Substitution, risk aversion, and the temporal behavior of consumption and asset returns: A theoretical framework, *Econometrica* **57**(4): 937–969.

Erev, I. and Roth, A. E. (1998). Predicting how people play games: Reinforcement learning in experimental games with unique, mixed strategy equilibria, *American Economic Review* **88**(4): 848–881.

Fabre, J. and Frino, A. (2004). Commonality in liquidity: Evidence from the Australian Stock Exchange, *Accounting & Finance* **44**(3): 357–368.

Faleye, O., Hoitash, R. and Hoitash, U. (2011). The costs of intense board monitoring, *Journal of Financial Economics* **101**(1): 160–181.

Falkenstein, E. G. (1996). Preferences for stock characteristics as revealed by mutual fund portfolio holdings, *The Journal of Finance* **51**(1): 111–135.

Fama, E. F. and French, K. R. (1988). Dividend yields and expected stock returns, *Journal of Financial Economics* **22**(1): 3–25.

Fama, E. F. and French, K. R. (1993). Common risk factors in the returns on stocks and bonds, *Journal of Financial Economics* **33**(1): 3–56.

Fama, E. F. and French, K. R. (1996). Multifactor explanations of asset pricing anomalies, *The Journal of Finance* **51**(1): 55–84.

Fama, E. F. and French, K. R. (1997). Industry costs of equity, *Journal of Financial Economics* **43**(2): 153–193.

Fama, E. F. and MacBeth, J. D. (1973). Risk, return, and equilibrium: Empirical tests, *Journal of Political Economy* **81**(3): 607–636.

Fang, V. W., Noe, T. H. and Tice, S. (2009). Stock market liquidity and firm value, *Journal of Financial Economics* **94**(1): 150–169.

Favara, G., Schroth, E. and Valta, P. (2012). Strategic default and equity risk across countries, *The Journal of Finance* **67**(6): 2051–2095.

Feng, L. and Seasholes, M. S. (2004). *Correlated trading and location,* **59**(5): 2117–2144.

Ferris, S. P. and Yan, X. S. (2009). Agency costs, governance, and organizational forms: evidence from the mutual fund industry, *Journal of Banking & Finance* **33**(4): 619–626.

Ferson, W. E. (2010). Investment performance evaluation, *Annual Review of Financial Economics* **2**(1): 207–234.

Field, L. C. and Lowry, M. (2009). Institutional versus individual investment in IPOs: The importance of firm fundamentals, *Journal of Financial and Quantitative Analysis* **44**(3): 489–516.

Fishman, M. J. and Hagerty, K. M. (1989). Disclosure decisions by firms and the competition for price efficiency, *The Journal of Finance* **44**(3): 633–646.

Folta, T. B. and Janney, J. J. (2004). Strategic benefits to firms issuing private equity placements, *Strategic Management Journal* **25**(3): 223–242.

Foster, F. D. and Viswanathan, S. (1993). The effect of public information and competition on trading volume and price volatility, *Review of Financial Studies* **6**(1): 23 –56.

Foster, F. D. and Viswanathan, S. (1994). Strategic trading with asymmetrically informed traders and long-lived information, *Journal of Financial and Quantitative Analysis* **29**(4): 499–518.

Foster, F. D. and Viswanathan, S. (1996). Strategic trading when agents forecast the forecasts of others, *The Journal of Finance* **51**(4): 1437–1478.

Foucault, T., Kadan, O. and Kandel, E. (2005). Limit order book as a market for liquidity, *Review of Financial Studies* **18**(4): 1171–1217.

Frank, M. Z. and Goyal, V. K. (2003). Testing the pecking order theory of capital structure, *Journal of Financial Economics* **67**(2): 217–248.

Franzoni, F., Nowak, E. and Phalippou, L. (2012). Private equity performance and liquidity risk, *The Journal of Finance* **67**(6): 2341–2373.

Frazzini, A. and Lamont, O. A. (2008). Dumb money: Mutual fund flows and the cross-section of stock returns, *Journal of Financial Economics* **88**(2): 299–322.

French, K. R. and Poterba, J. M. (1991). Investor diversification and international equity markets, *American Economic Review* **81**(2): 222–226.

Frieder, L. and Subrahmanyam, A. (2005). Brand perceptions and the market for common stock, *Journal of Financial and Quantitative Analysis* **40**(1): 57– 85.

Friedman, B. M. (1979). Optimal expectations and the extreme information assumptions of 'rational expectations' macromodels, *Journal of Monetary Economics* **5**(1): 23–41.

Froot, K. A., O'Connell, P. G. J. and Seasholes, M. S. (2001). The portfolio flows of international investors, *Journal of Financial Economics* **59**(2): 151–193.

Froot, K. A., Scharfstein, D. S. and Stein, J. C. (1992). Herd on the street: Informational inefficiencies in a market with short-term speculation, *The Journal of Finance* **47**(4): 1461–1484.

Fudenberg, D. and Tirole, J. (1991). *Game theory*. The MIT Press, Cambridge, Massachusetts.

García, D. and Vanden, J. M. (2009). Information acquisition and mutual funds, *Journal of Economic Theory* **144**(5): 1965–1995.

Garman, M. B. (1976). Market microstructure, *Journal of Financial Economics* **3**(3): 257–275.

Gibson, S., Safieddine, A. and Sonti, R. (2004). Smart investments by smart money: Evidence from seasoned equity offerings, *Journal of Financial Economics* **72**(3): 581–604.

Gil-Bazo, J. and Ruiz-Verd, P. (2008). When cheaper is better: Fee determination in the market for equity mutual funds, *Journal of Economic Behavior & Organization* **67**(34): 871–885.

Gil-Bazo, J. and Ruiz-Verd, P. (2009). The relation between price and performance in the mutual fund industry, *The Journal of Finance* **64**(5): 2153–2183.

Gilboa, I. and Schmeidler, D. (1989). Maxmin expected utility with non-unique prior, *Journal of Mathematical Economics* **18**(2): 141–153.

Glosten, L. R. (1989). Insider trading, liquidity, and the role of the monopolist specialist, *The Journal of Business* **62**(2): 211–235.

Glosten, L. R. (1994). Is the electronic open limit order book inevitable?, *The Journal of Finance* **49**(4): 1127–1161.

Glosten, L. R. and Harris, L. E. (1988). Estimating the components of the bid/ask spread, *Journal of Financial Economics* **21**(1): 123–142.

Glosten, L. R. and Milgrom, P. R. (1985). Bid, ask and transaction prices in a specialist market with heterogeneously informed traders, *Journal of Financial Economics* **14**(1): 71–100.

Goettler, R. L., Parlour, C. A. and Rajan, U. (2005). Equilibrium in a dynamic limit order market, *The Journal of Finance* **60**(5): 2149–2192.

Goettler, R. L., Parlour, C. A. and Rajan, U. (2009). Informed traders and limit order markets, *Journal of Financial Economics* **93**(1): 67–87.

Goetzmann, W., Ingersoll, J., Spiegel, M. and Welch, I. (2007). Portfolio performance manipulation and manipulation-proof performance measures, *Review of Financial Studies* **20**(5): 1503 –1546.

Goetzmann, W. N. and Ibbotson, R. G. (1994). Do winners repeat? patterns in mutual fund behavior, *Journal of Portfolio Management* **20**(2): 9–18.

Goetzmann, W. N. and Peles, N. (1997). Cognitive dissonance and mutual fund investors, *Journal of Financial Research* **20**(2): 145.

Goetzmann, W. N. and Zhu, N. (2005). Rain or shine: Where is the weather effect?, *European Financial Management* **11**(5): 559–578.

Goldstein, M. A., Irvine, P. and Puckett, A. (2011). Purchasing IPOs with commissions, *Journal of Financial and Quantitative Analysis* **46**(5): 1193– 1225.

Golec, J. and Starks, L. (2004). Performance fee contract change and mutual fund risk, *Journal of Financial Economics* **73**(1): 93–118.

Gompers, P. A. and Metrick, A. (2001). Institutional investors and equity prices, *The Quarterly Journal of Economics* **116**(1): 229–259.

Good, W. R., Ferguson, R. and Treynor, J. (1976). An investor's guide to the index fund controversy, *Financial Analysts Journal* **32**(6): 27–36.

Goriaev, A., Nijman, T. E. and Werker, B. J. M. (2005). Yet another look at mutual fund tournaments, *Journal of Empirical Finance* **12**(1): 127–137.

Goyenko, R. Y., Holden, C. W. and Trzcinka, C. A. (2009). Do liquidity measures measure liquidity?, *Journal of Financial Economics* **92**(2): 153–181.

Greenwood, R. and Nagel, S. (2009). Inexperienced investors and bubbles, *Journal of Financial Economics* **93**(2): 239–258.

Griffin, J. M., Harris, J. H. and Topaloglu, S. (2003). The dynamics of institutional and individual trading, *The Journal of Finance* **58**(6): 2285–2320.

Grinblatt, M. and Keloharju, M. (2000). The investment behavior and performance of various investor types: A study of Finland's unique data set, *Journal of Financial Economics* **55**(1): 43–67.

Grinblatt, M. and Keloharju, M. (2001a). How distance, language, and culture influence stockholdings and trades, *The Journal of Finance* **56**(3): 1053–1073.

Grinblatt, M. and Keloharju, M. (2001b). What makes investors trade?, *The Journal of Finance* **56**(2): 589–616.

Grinblatt, M. S. and Ross, S. A. (1985). Market power in a securities market with endogenous information, *The Quarterly Journal of Economics* **100**(4): 1143–1167.

Grinblatt, M. and Titman, S. (1989). Adverse risk incentives and the design of performance-based contracts, *Management Science* **35**(7): 807–822.

Grinblatt, M. and Titman, S. (1992). The persistence of mutual fund performance, *The Journal of Finance* **47**(5): 1977–1984.

Grinblatt, M. and Titman, S. (1993). Performance measurement without benchmarks: An examination of mutual fund returns, *The Journal of Business* **66**(1): 47–68.

Grinblatt, M., Titman, S. and Wermers, R. (1995). Momentum investment strategies, portfolio performance, and herding: A study of mutual fund behavior, *American Economic Review* **85**(5): 1088–1105.

Gromb, D. and Vayanos, D. (2002). Equilibrium and welfare in markets with financially constrained arbitrageurs, *Journal of Financial Economics* **66**(23): 361–407.

Gromb, D. and Vayanos, D. (2010). Limits of arbitrage, *Annual Review of Financial Economics* **2**(1): 251–275.

Grossman, S. (1976). On the efficiency of competitive stock markets where trades have diverse information, *The Journal of Finance* **31**(2): 573–585.

Grossman, S. J. (1981). An introduction to the theory of rational expectations under asymmetric information, *Review of Economic Studies* **48**(4): 541 –559.

Gruber, M. J. (1996). Another puzzle: The growth in actively managed mutual funds, *The Journal of Finance* **51**(3): 783–810.

Grullon, G., Kanatas, G. and Weston, J. P. (2004). Advertising, breadth of ownership, and liquidity, *Review of Financial Studies* **17**(2): 439–461.

Grundy, B. D. and Kim, Y. (2002). Stock market volatility in a heterogeneous information economy, *Journal of Financial and Quantitative Analysis* **37**(1): 1–27.

Grundy, B. D. and McNichols, M. (1989). Trade and the revelation of information through prices and direct disclosure, *Review of Financial Studies* **2**(4): 495 –526.

Guiso, L., Sapienza, P. and Zingales, L. (2008). Does local financial development matter?, Working Paper .

Guo, S., Hotchkiss, E. S. and Song, W. (2011). Do buyouts (still) create value?, *The Journal of Finance* **66**(2): 479–517.

Hameed, A., Kang, W. and Viswanathan, S. (2010). Stock market declines and liquidity, *The Journal of Finance* **65**(1): 257–293.

Hanley, K. W. (1993). The underpricing of initial public offerings and the partial adjustment phenomenon, *Journal of Financial Economics* **34**(2): 231–250.

Harless, D. W. and Peterson, S. P. (1998). Investor behavior and the persistence of poorly-performing mutual funds, *Journal of Economic Behavior & Organization* **37**(3): 257–276.

Harris, J. H. and Schultz, P. H. (1998). The trading profits of SOES bandits, *Journal of Financial Economics* **50**(1): 39–62.

Harris, L. (1998). Optimal dynamic order submission strategies in some stylized trading problems, Financial Markets, *Institutions & Instruments* **7**(2): 1–76.

Harris, L. E. and Panchapagesan, V. (2005). The information content of the limit order book: evidence from NYSE specialist trading decisions, *Journal of Financial Markets* **8**(1): 25–67.

Harrison, J. M. and Kreps, D. M. (1978). Speculative investor behavior in a stock market with heterogeneous expectations, *The Quarterly Journal of Economics* **92**(2): 323–336.

Hartzmark, M. L. (1991). Luck versus forecast ability: Determinants of trader performance in futures markets, *The Journal of Business* **64**(1): 49–74.

Haruvy, E., Lahav, Y. and Noussair, C. N. (2007). Traders' expectations in asset markets: Experimental evidence, *American Economic Review* **97**(5): 1901– 1920.

Hasbrouck, J. (1988). Trades, quotes, inventories, and information, *Journal of Financial Economics* **22**(2): 229–252.

Hasbrouck, J. (1991a). Measuring the information content of stock trades, *The Journal of Finance* **46**(1): 179–207.

Hasbrouck, J. (1991b). The summary informativeness of stock trades: An econometric analysis, *Review of Financial Studies* **4**(3): 571–595.

Hasbrouck, J. (1995). One security, many markets: Determining the contributions to price discovery, *The Journal of Finance* **50**(4): 1175–1199.

Hasbrouck, J. (1999). The dynamics of discrete bid and ask quotes, *The Journal of Finance* **54**(6): 2109–2142.

Hasbrouck, J. (2003). Intraday price formation in U.S. equity index markets,

The Journal of Finance **58**(6): 2375–2399.

Hasbrouck, J. and Saar, G. (2009). Technology and liquidity provision: The blurring of traditional definitions, *Journal of Financial Markets* **12**(2): 143– 172.

Hasbrouck, J. and Seppi, D. J. (2001). Common factors in prices, order flows, and liquidity, *Journal of Financial Economics* **59**(3): 383–411.

Hasbrouck, J. and Sofianos, G. (1993). The trades of market makers: An empirical analysis of NYSE specialists, *The Journal of Finance* **48**(5): 1565–1593.

Hausman, J. A., Lo, A. W. and MacKinlay, A. C. (1992). An ordered probit analysis of transaction stock prices, *Journal of Financial Economics* **31**(3): 319–379.

Hayek, F. A. (1945). The use of knowledge in society, *American Economic Review* **35**(4): 519–530.

He, J. J., Qian, J. Q. and Strahan, P. E. (2012). Are all ratings created equal? The impact of issuer size on the pricing of mortgage-backed securities, *The Journal of Finance* **67**(6): 2097–2137.

Heckman, J. J. (1979). Sample selection bias as a specification error, *Econometrica* **47**(1): 153–161.

Heflin, F. and Shaw, K. W. (2000). Blockholder ownership and market liquidity, *Journal of Financial and Quantitative Analysis* **35**(4): 621–633.

Heidle, H. G. and Huang, R. D. (2002). Information-based trading in dealer and auction markets: An analysis of exchange listings, *Journal of Financial and Quantitative Analysis* **37**(3): 391–424.

Heinkel, R. and Stoughton, N. M. (1994). The dynamics of portfolio management contracts, *Review of Financial Studies* **7**(2): 351–387.

Hellwig, M. F. (1980). On the aggregation of information in competitive markets, *Journal of Economic Theory* **22**(3): 477–498.

Hendershott, T., Jones, C. M. and Menkveld, A. J. (2011). Does algorithmic trading improve liquidity?, *The Journal of Finance* **66**(1): 1–33.

Hendricks, D., Patel, J. and Zeckhauser, R. (1993). Hot hands in mutual funds: Short-run persistence of relative performance, 1974-1988, *The Journal of Finance* **48**(1): 93–130.

Henry, T. R. and Koski, J. L. (2010). Short selling around seasoned equity offerings, *Review of Financial Studies*(12): 4389 –4418.

Hertzel, M., Lemmon, M., Linck, J. S. and Rees, L. (2002). Long-run performance following private placements of equity, *The Journal of Finance* **57**(6): 2595–2617.

Hertzel, M. and Rees, L. (1998). Earnings and risk changes around private placements of equity, Journal of Accounting, *Auditing & Finance* **13**(1): 21– 35.

Hertzel, M. and Smith, R. L. (1993). Market discounts and shareholder gains for placing equity privately, *The Journal of Finance* **48**(2): 459–485.

Hirshleifer, D. and Luo, G. Y. (2001). On the survival of overconfident traders in a competitive securities market, *Journal of Financial Markets* **4**(1): 73–84.

Hirshleifer, D., Subrahmanyam, A. and Titman, S. (1994). Security analysis and trading patterns when some investors receive information before others, *The Journal of Finance* **49**(5): 1665–1698.

Ho, T. and Stoll, H. R. (1981). Optimal dealer pricing under transactions and return uncertainty, *Journal of Financial Economics* **9**(1): 47–73.

Hoechle, D., Schmid, M., Walter, I. and Yermack, D. (2012). How much of the diversification discount can be explained by poor corporate governance?, *Journal of Financial Economics* **103**(1): 41–60.

Holden, C. W. and Subrahmanyam, A. (1992). Long-lived private information and imperfect competition, *The Journal of Finance* **47**(1): 247–270.

Holden, C. W. and Subrahmanyam, A. (1994). Risk aversion, imperfect competition, and long-lived information, *Economics Letters* **44**(12): 181–190.

Holmström, B. and Tirole, J. (1993). Market liquidity and performance monitoring, *Journal of Political Economy* **101**(4): 678–709.

Hong, H. and Kostovetsky, L. (2012). Red and blue investing: Values and finance, *Journal of Financial Economics* **103**(1): 1–19.

Hong, H. and Stein, J. C. (1999). A unified theory of underreaction, momentum trading, and overreaction in asset markets, *The Journal of Finance* **54**(6): 2143–2184.

Hong, H. and Stein, J. C. (2003). Differences of opinion, short-sales constraints, and market crashes, *Review of Financial Studies* **16**(2): 487 –525.

Hovakimian, A., Hovakimian, G. and Tehranian, H. (2004). Determinants of target capital structure: The case of dual debt and equity issues, *Journal of Financial Economics* **71**(3): 517–540.

Hovakimian, A. and Li, G. (2011). In search of conclusive evidence: How to test for adjustment to target capital structure, *Journal of Corporate Finance* **17**(1): 33–44.

Hovakimian, A., Opler, T. and Titman, S. (2001). The debt-equity choice, *Journal of Financial and Quantitative Analysis* **36**(1): 1–24.

Huang, R. D. (2002). The quality of ECN and NASDAQ market maker quotes, *The Journal of Finance* **57**(3): 1285–1319.

Huang, R. D. and Stoll, H. R. (1996). Dealer versus auction markets: A paired comparison of execution costs on NASDAQ and the NYSE, *Journal of Financial Economics* **41**(3): 313–357.

Huang, R. D. and Stoll, H. R. (1997). The components of the bid-ask spread: A general approach, *Review of Financial Studies* **10**(4): 995–1034.

Huberman, G. and Halka, D. (2001). Systematic liquidity, *Journal of Financial Research* **24**(2): 161–178.

Huberman, G. and Kandel, S. (1993). On the incentives for money managers: A signalling approach, *European Economic Review* **37**(5): 1065–1081.

Huddart, S. (1999). Reputation and performance fee effects on portfolio choice by investment advisers, *Journal of Financial Markets* **2**(3): 227–271.

Hughes, J. S., Liu, J. and Liu, J. (2007). Information asymmetry, diversification, and cost of capital, *Accounting Review* **82**(3): 705–730.

Hwang, L.-S., Lee, W.-J., Lim, S.-Y. and Park, K.-H. (2013). Does information risk affect the implied cost of equity capital? An analysis of PIN and adjusted PIN, *Journal of Accounting and Economics* **55**(2¨C3): 148–167.

Indro, D. C., Jiang, C. X., Hu, M. Y. and Lee, W. Y. (1999). Mutual fund performance: Does fund size matter?, *Financial Analysts Journal* **55**(3): 74– 87.

Ingersoll, J. E. and Jin, L. J. (2013). Realization utility with reference-dependent preferences, *Review of Financial Studies* **26**(3): 723 –767.

Ippolito, R. A. (1992). Consumer reaction to measures of poor quality: evidence from the mutual fund industry, *Journal of Law and Economics* **35**(1): 45–70.

Jain, P. C. and Wu, J. S. (2000). Truth in mutual fund advertising: Evidence on future performance and fund flows, *The Journal of Finance* **55**(2): 937–958.

Jang, H. and Venkatesh, P. C. (1991). Consistency between predicted and actual bid-ask quote-revisions, *The Journal of Finance* **46**(1): 433–446.

Jegadeesh, N. (1990). Evidence of predictable behavior of security returns, *The Journal of Finance* **45**(3): 881–898.

Jegadeesh, N. and Titman, S. (1993). Returns to buying winners and selling losers: Implications for stock market efficiency, *The Journal of Finance* **48**(1): 65–91.

Jegadeesh, N. and Titman, S. (1995). Short-horizon return reversals and the bid-ask spread, *Journal of Financial Intermediation* **4**(2): 116–132.

Jegadeesh, N. and Titman, S. (2001). Profitability of momentum strategies: An evaluation of alternative explanations, *The Journal of Finance* **56**(2): 699– 720.

Jensen, M. C. (1968). The performance of mutual funds in the period 1945-1964, *The Journal of Finance* **23**(2): 389–416.

Jeremy, L. (2007). Measuring the resiliency of an electronic limit order book, *Journal of Financial Markets* **10**(1): 1–25.

Johnson, S. A., Lin, J.-C. and Roy Song, K. (2006). Dividend policy, signaling, and discounts on closed-end funds, *Journal of Financial Economics* **81**(3): 539–562.

Judd, K. L., Kubler, F. and Schmedders, K. (2003). Asset trading volume with dynamically complete markets and heterogeneous agents, *The Journal of Finance* **58**(5): 2203–2218.

Kahneman, D. and Tversky, A. (1979). Prospect theory: An analysis of decision under risk, *Econometrica* **47**(2): 263–291.

Kamara, A., Lou, X. and Sadka, R. (2008). The divergence of liquidity commonality in the cross-section of stocks, *Journal of Financial Economics* **89**(3): 444–466.

Kandel, E. and Pearson, N. D. (1995). Differential interpretation of public signals and trade in speculative markets, *Journal of Political Economy* **103**(4):

831–872.

Kang, Q. and Liu, Q. (2008). Stock trading, information production, and executive incentives, *Journal of Corporate Finance* **14**(4): 484–498.

Kaniel, R. and Liu, H. (2006). So what orders do informed traders use?, *The Journal of Business* **79**(4): 1867–1913.

Karpoff, J. M. (1987). The relation between price changes and trading volume: A survey, *Journal of Financial and Quantitative Analysis* **22**(1): 109–126.

Kaul, G. and Nimalendran, M. (1990). Price reversals: Bid-ask errors or market overreaction?, *Journal of Financial Economics* **28**(1¨C2): 67–93.

Kaustia, M. and Knüpfer, S. (2008). Do investors overweight personal experience? Evidence from IPO subscriptions, *The Journal of Finance* **63**(6): 2679– 2702.

Kavajecz, K. A. and Odders-White, E. R. (2004). Technical analysis and liquidity provision, *Review of Financial Studies* **17**(4): 1043–1071.

Kedia, S. and Panchapagesan, V. (2011). Why do only some NASDAQ firms switch to the NYSE? Evidence from corporate transactions, *Journal of Financial Markets* **14**(1): 109–126.

Kehr, C.-H., Krahnen, J. P. and Theissen, E. (2001). The anatomy of a call market, *Journal of Financial Intermediation* **10**(3¨C4): 249–270.

Keim, D. B. (1999). An analysis of mutual fund design: the case of investing in small-cap stocks, *Journal of Financial Economics* **51**(2): 173–194.

Keim, D. B. and Madhavan, A. (1995). Anatomy of the trading process empirical evidence on the behavior of institutional traders, *Journal of Financial Economics* **37**(3): 371–398.

Keim, D. B. and Madhavan, A. (1996). The upstairs market for large-block transactions: Analysis and measurement of price effects, *Review of Financial Studies* **9**(1): 1–36.

Keller, M. C., Fredrickson, B. L., Ybarra, O., Côté, S., Johnson, K., Mikels, J., Conway, A. and Wager, T. (2005). A warm heart and a clear head: The contingent effects of weather on mood and cognition, *Psychological Science* **16**(9): 724–731.

Kelly, B. and Ljungqvist, A. (2012). Testing asymmetric-information asset pricing models, *Review of Financial Studies* **25**(5): 1366 –1413.

Keswani, A. and Stolin, D. (2008). Which money is smart? Mutual fund buys and sells of individual and institutional investors, *The Journal of Finance* **63**(1): 85–118.

Keynes, J. M. (1936). The General Theory of Employment, Interest and Money Macmillan, London.

Khandani, A. E. and Lo, A. W. (2011). What happened to the quants in August 2007? Evidence from factors and transactions data, *Journal of Financial Markets* **14**(1): 1–46.

Khorana, A., Servaes, H. and Tufano, P. (2005). Explaining the size of the mutual fund industry around the world, *Journal of Financial Economics* **78**(1):

145–185.

Khorana, A., Servaes, H. and Tufano, P. (2009). Mutual fund fees around the world, *Review of Financial Studies* **22**(3): 1279–1310.

Kim, K. A. and Shin, H.-H. (2004). The puzzling increase in the underpricing of seasoned equity offerings, *Financial Review* **39**(3): 343–365.

Kim, O. and Verrecchia, R. E. (1991a). Market reaction to anticipated announcements, *Journal of Financial Economics* **30**(2): 273–309.

Kim, O. and Verrecchia, R. E. (1991b). Trading volume and price reactions to public announcements, *Journal of Accounting Research* **29**(2): 302–321.

Kim, S. T. (2013). The timing of opening trades and pricing errors, *Financial Management* **42**(3): 503–516.

Kim, W. and Weisbach, M. S. (2008). Motivations for public equity offers: An international perspective, *Journal of Financial Economics* **87**(2): 281–307.

King, M. R. (2009). Prebid run-ups ahead of Canadian takeovers: How big is the problem?, *Financial Management* **38**(4): 699–726.

Klibanoff, P., Marinacci, M. and Mukerji, S. (2005). A smooth model of decision making under ambiguity, *Econometrica* **73**(6): 1849–1892.

Kliger, D., Levy, O. and Sonsino, D. (2003). On absolute and relative performance and the demand for mutual funds–experimental evidence, *Journal of Economic Behavior & Organization* **52**(3): 341–363.

Knetsch, J. L. and Sinden, J. A. (1984). Willingness to pay and compensation demanded: Experimental evidence of an unexpected disparity in measures of value, *The Quarterly Journal of Economics* **99**(3): 507 –521.

Knyazeva, A., Knyazeva, D. and Masulis, R. W. (2009). Local director talent and board composition, Working Paper .

Korajczyk, R. A. and Sadka, R. (2008). Pricing the commonality across alternative measures of liquidity, *Journal of Financial Economics* **87**(1): 45–72.

Korteweg, A. and Sorensen, M. (2010). Risk and return characteristics of venture capital-backed entrepreneurial companies, *Review of Financial Studies* **23**(10): 3738 –3772.

Koski, J. L. and Pontiff, J. (1999). How are derivatives used? evidence from the mutual fund industry, *The Journal of Finance* **54**(2): 791–816.

Krishnan, C. N. V., Ivanov, V. I., Masulis, R. W. and Singh, A. K. (2011). Venture capital reputation, post-IPO performance, and corporate governance, *Journal of Financial and Quantitative Analysis* **46**(5): 1295–1333.

Kuhn, P. and Shen, K. (2013). Gender discrimination in job ads: Evidence from China, *The Quarterly Journal of Economics* **128(**1): 287 –336.

Kuhnen, C. M. (2009). Business networks, corporate governance, and contracting in the mutual fund industry, *The Journal of Finance* **64**(5): 2185–2220.

Kumar, A. and Lee, C. M. C. (2006). Retail investor sentiment and return comovements, *The Journal of Finance* **61**(5): 2451–2486.

Kurov, A. and Lasser, D. J. (2004). Price dynamics in the regular and E-Mini futures markets, *Journal of Financial and Quantitative Analysis* **39**(2): 365– 384.

Kyle, A. S. (1985). Continuous auctions and insider trading, *Econometrica* **53**(6): 1315–1335.

Kyle, A. S. and Wang, F. A. (1997). Speculation duopoly with agreement to disagree: Can overconfidence survive the market test?, *The Journal of Finance* **52**(5): 2073–2090.

Kyle, A. S. and Xiong, W. (2001). Contagion as a wealth effect, *The Journal of Finance* **56**(4): 1401–1440.

Lakonishok, J., Shleifer, A. and Vishny, R. W. (1992). The impact of institutional trading on stock prices, *Journal of Financial Economics* **32**(1): 23–43.

Lakonishok, J., Shleifer, A. and Vishny, R. W. (1994). Contrarian investment, extrapolation, and risk, *The Journal of Finance* **49**(5): 1541–1578.

Lambert, R. A., Leuz, C. and Verrecchia, R. E. (2012). Information asymmetry, information precision, and the cost of capital, *Review of Finance* **16**(1): 1 –29.

Lambert, R., Leuz, C. and Verrecchia, R. E. (2007). Accounting information, disclosure, and the cost of capital, *Journal of Accounting Research* **45**(2): 385–420.

Lamont, O. A. (2000). Investment plans and stock returns, *The Journal of Finance* **55**(6): 2719–2745.

Lamont, O. A. (2012). Go down fighting: Short sellers vs. firms, *Review of Asset Pricing Studies* **2**(1): 1 –30.

Lamont, O. A. and Thaler, R. H. (2003). Can the market add and subtract? Mispricing in tech stock carve-outs, *Journal of Political Economy* **111**(2): 227–268.

Lamoureux, C. G. and Lastrapes, W. D. (1990). Heteroskedasticity in stock return data: Volume versus GARCH effects, *The Journal of Finance* **45**(1): 221–229.

LaPlante, M. and Muscarella, C. J. (1997). Do institutions receive comparable execution in the NYSE and Nasdaq markets? A transaction study of block trades, *Journal of Financial Economics* **45**(1): 97–134.

Leary, M. T. and Roberts, M. R. (2005). Do firms rebalance their capital structures?, *The Journal of Finance* **60**(6): 2575–2619.

Lease, R. C., Masulis, R. W. and Page, J. R. (1991). An investigation of market microstructure impacts on event study returns, *The Journal of Finance* **46**(4): 1523–1536.

Lee, D. S. and Lemieux, T. (2010). Regression discontinuity designs in economics, *Journal of Economic Literature* **48**(2): 281–355.

Lee, K.-H. (2011). The world price of liquidity risk, *Journal of Financial Economics* (1): 136–161.

Lehmann, B. N. (1990). Fads, martingales, and market efficiency, *The Quarterly Journal of Economics* **105**(1): 1–28.

Lemmon, M. L., Roberts, M. R. and Zender, J. F. (2008). Back to the beginning: Persistence and the cross-section of corporate capital structure, *The Journal of Finance* **63**(4): 1575–1608.

Lemmon, M. L. and Zender, J. F. (2010). Debt capacity and tests of capital structure theories, *Journal of Financial and Quantitative Analysis* **45**(5): 1161–1187.

Lesmond, D. A., Ogden, J. P. and Trzcinka, C. A. (1999). A new estimate of transaction costs, *Review of Financial Studies* **12**(5): 1113–1141.

Lewellen, J., Nagel, S. and Shanken, J. (2010). A skeptical appraisal of asset pricing tests, *Journal of Financial Economics* **96**(2): 175–194.

Li, E. X. N., Livdan, D. and Zhang, L. (2009). Anomalies, *Review of Financial Studies* **22**(11): 4301–4334.

Li, H., Zhang, X. and Zhao, R. (2011). Investing in talents: Manager characteristics and hedge fund performances, *Journal of Financial and Quantitative Analysis* **46**(1): 59–82.

Li, K. and Prabhala, N. R. (2007). Self-selection models in corporate finance, in B. E. Eckbo (ed.), Handbook of Empirical Corporate Finance, 1 edn, Vol. 1, pp. 39–86.

Linnainmaa, J. T. (2010). Do limit orders alter inferences about investor performance and behavior?, *The Journal of Finance* **65**(4): 1473–1506.

Linnainmaa, J. T. and Saar, G. (2012). Lack of anonymity and the inference from order flow, Review of Financial Studies .

Lipson, M. L. and Mortal, S. (2009). Liquidity and capital structure, *Journal of Financial Markets* **12**(4): 611–644.

List, J. A. (2003). Does market experience eliminate market anomalies?, *The Quarterly Journal of Economics* **118**(1): 41 –71.

Liu, W.-M. (2009). Monitoring and limit order submission risks, *Journal of Financial Markets* **12**(1): 107–141.

Liu, W. and Strong, N. (2008). Biases in decomposing holding-period portfolio returns, *Review of Financial Studies* **21**(5): 2243 –2274.

Liu, X. and Ritter, J. R. (2011). Local underwriter oligopolies and IPO underpricing, *Journal of Financial Economics* **102**(3): 579–601.

Llorente, G., Michaely, R., Gideon, S. and Wang, J. (2002). Dynamic volumereturn relation of individual stocks, *Review of Financial Studies* **15**(4): 1005– 1047.

Lo, A. W. and MacKinlay, A. C. (1988). Stock market prices do not follow random walks: Evidence from a simple specification test, *Review of Financial Studies* **1**(1): 41–66.

Lo, A. W. and Wang, J. (2000). Trading volume: Definitions, data analysis, and implications of portfolio theory, *Review of Financial Studies* **13**(2): 257–300.

Loughran, T. and Ritter, J. R. (1997). The operating performance of firms conducting seasoned equity offerings, *The Journal of Finance* **52**(5): 1823– 1850.

Loughran, T. and Schultz, P. (2005). Liquidity: Urban versus rural firms,

Journal of Financial Economics **78**(2): 341–374.

Lundeberg, M. A., Fox, P. W. and Punćochar, J. (1994). Highly confident but wrong: Gender differences and similarities in confidence judgments, *Journal of Educational Psychology* **86**(1): 114–121.

Luo, G. Y. (2002). Mutual fund fee-setting, market structure and mark-ups, *Economica* **69**(274): 245–271.

Lynch, A. W. and Musto, D. K. (2003). How investors interpret past fund returns, *The Journal of Finance* **58**(5): 2033–2058.

Madhavan, A. (1992). Trading mechanisms in securities markets, *The Journal of Finance* **47**(2): 607–641.

Madhavan, A. and Panchapagesan, V. (2000). Price discovery in auction markets: A look inside the black box, *Review of Financial Studies* **13**(3): 627 –658.

Madhavan, A. and Panchapagesan, V. (2002). The first price of the day, *Journal of Portfolio Management* **28**(2): 101–111.

Madhavan, A., Richardson, M. and Roomans, M. (1997). Why do security prices change? A transaction-level analysis of NYSE stocks, *Review of Financial Studies* **10**(4): 1035–1064.

Madhavan, A. and Smidt, S. (1993). An analysis of changes in specialist inventories and quotations, *The Journal of Finance* **48**(5): 1595–1628.

Malherbe, F. (2011). Self-fulfilling liquidity dry-ups, Working Paper .

Malhotra, D. K. and Mcleod, R. W. (1997). An empirical analysis of mutual fund expenses, *Journal of Financial Research* **20**(2): 175–190.

Malmendier, U. and Nagel, S. (2011). Depression babies: Do macroeconomic experiences affect risk taking?, *The Quarterly Journal of Economics* **126**(1): 373 –416.

Malmendier, U. and Tate, G. (2005). CEO overconfidence and corporate investment, *The Journal of Finance* **60**(6): 2661–2700.

Manaster, S., Mann, S. C. and Abarbanell, J. (1999). Sources of market making profits: Man does not live by spread alone, Working Paper .

Manove, M. (1989). The harm from insider trading and informed speculation, *The Quarterly Journal of Economics* **104**(4): 823–845.

Mas-Colell, A., Green, J. R. and Whinston, M. D. (1995). Microeconomic theory Oxford University Press, New York.

Massa, M. and Patgiri, R. (2009). Incentives and mutual fund performance: higher performance or just higher risk taking?, *Review of Financial Studies* **22**(5): 1777–1815.

Masulis, R. W. and Kim, S. (2010). Order imbalances around seasoned equity offerings, SSRN eLibrary .

Masulis, R. W. and Korwar, A. N. (1986). Seasoned equity offerings: An empirical investigation, *Journal of Financial Economics* **15**(12): 91–118.

Masulis, R. W. and Mobbs, S. (2011). Are all inside directors the same?

Evidence from the external directorship market, *The Journal of Finance* **66**(3): 823– 872.

Masulis, R. W. and Shivakumar, L. (2002). Does market structure affect the immediacy of stock price responses to news?, *Journal of Financial and Quantitative Analysis* **37**(4): 617–648.

Masulis, R. W., Wang, C. and Xie, F. (2011). Globalizing the boardroom—the effects of foreign directors on corporate governance and firm performance, SSRN eLibrary .

McLaughlin, R., Safieddine, A. and Vasudevan, G. K. (1996). The operating performance of seasoned equity issuers: Free cash flow and post-issue performance, *Financial Management* **25**(4): 41–53.

Mendelson, H. and Tunca, T. I. (2004). Strategic trading, liquidity, and information acquisition, *Review of Financial Studies* **17**(2): 295–337.

Menkhoff, L. and Schmeling, M. (2010). Whose trades convey information? evidence from a cross-section of traders, *Journal of Financial Markets* **13**(1): 101–128.

Merton, R. C. (1987). A simple model of capital market equilibrium with incomplete information, *The Journal of Finance* **42**(3): 483–510.

Milgrom, P. R. (1981). Good news and bad news: Representation theorems and applications, *The Bell Journal of Economics* **12**(2): 380–391.

Milgrom, P. and Stokey, N. (1982). Information, trade and common knowledge, *Journal of Economic Theory* **26**(1): 17–27.

Miller, E. M. (1977). Risk, uncertainty, and divergence of opinion, *The Journal of Finance* **32**(4): 1151–1168.

Miller, M. H. and Rock, K. (1985). Dividend policy under asymmetric information, *The Journal of Finance* **40**(4): 1031–1051.

Milton, H. and Raviv, A. (1993). Differences of opinion make a horse race, *Review of Financial Studies* **6**(3): 473–506.

Mitchell, M., Pedersen, L. H. and Pulvino, T. (2007). Slow moving capital, *American Economic Review* **97**(2): 215–220.

Moeller, S. B., Schlingemann, F. P. and Stulz, R. M. (2007). How do diversity of opinion and information asymmetry affect acquirer returns?, *Review of Financial Studies* **20**(6): 2047–2078.

Mohanram, P. and Rajgopal, S. (2009). Is PIN priced risk?, *Journal of Accounting and Economics* **47**(3): 226–243.

Morck, R., Yeung, B. and Yu, W. (2000). The information content of stock markets: why do emerging markets have synchronous stock price movements?, *Journal of Financial Economics* **58**(12): 215–260.

Morris, S. (1996). Speculative investor behavior and learning, *The Quarterly Journal of Economics* **111**(4): 1111–1133.

Myers, S. C. and Majluf, N. S. (1984). Corporate financing and investment decisions when firms have information that investors do not have, *Journal of*

Financial Economics **13**(2): 187–221.

Næs, R., Skjeltorp, J. A. and Ødegaard, B. A. (2011). Stock market liquidity and the business cycle, *The Journal of Finance* **66**(1): 139–176.

Nagel, S. (2013). Empirical cross-sectional asset pricing, *Annual Review of Financial Economics* **5**(1): 167–199.

Nanda, V., Narayanan, M. P. and Warther, V. A. (2000). Liquidity, investment ability, and mutual fund structure, *Journal of Financial Economics* **57**(3): 417-443.

Nicolosi, G., Peng, L. and Zhu, N. (2009). Do individual investors learn from their trading experience?, *Journal of Financial Markets* **12**(2): 317–336.

Nofsinger, J. R. and Sias, R. W. (1999). Herding and feedback trading by institutional and individual investors, *The Journal of Finance* **54**(6): 2263– 2295.

Oberlechner, T. and Osler, C. (2012). Survival of overconfidence in currency markets, *Journal of Financial and Quantitative Analysis* **47**(1): 91–113.

Odders-White, E. R. and Ready, M. J. (2006). Credit ratings and stock liquidity, *Review of Financial Studies* **19**(1): 119–157.

Odean, T. (1998a). Are investors reluctant to realize their losses?, *The Journal of Finance* **53**(5): 1775–1798.

Odean, T. (1998b). Volume, volatility, price, and profit when all traders are above average, *The Journal of Finance* **53**(6): 1887–1934.

O'Hara, M. (2003). Presidential address: Liquidity and price discovery, *The Journal of Finance* **58**(4): 1335–1354.

O'Hara, M. and Oldfield, G. S. (1986). The microeconomics of market making, *Journal of Financial and Quantitative Analysis* **21**(4): 361–376.

Osborne, M. J. (2004). *An introduction to game theory*. Oxford University Press, New York.

Oyarzun, C. and Sarin, R. (2013). Learning and risk aversion, *Journal of Economic Theory* **148**(1): 196–225.

Öztekin, Ö. and Flannery, M. J. (2012). Institutional determinants of capital structure adjustment speeds, *Journal of Financial Economics* **103**(1): 88–112.

Pagano, M. and Volpin, P. F. (2010). Securitization, transparency and liquidity, *SSRN eLibrary* .

Panayides, M. A. (2007). Affirmative obligations and market making with inventory, *Journal of Financial Economics* **86**(2): 513–542.

Papay, J. P., Willett, J. B. and Murnane, R. J. (2011). Extending the regressiondiscontinuity approach to multiple assignment variables, *Journal of Econometrics* **161**(2): 203–207.

Parlour, C. A. (1998). Price dynamics in limit order markets, *Review of Financial Studies* **11**(4): 789–816.

Pástor, Ł. and Stambaugh, R. F. (2003). Liquidity risk and expected stock returns, *Journal of Political Economy* **111**(3): 642–685.

Pástor, Ł. and Veronesi, P. (2005). Rational IPO waves, *The Journal of*

Finance **60**(4): 1713–1757.

Pereira, J. P. and Zhang, H. H. (2010). Stock returns and the volatility of liquidity, *Journal of Financial and Quantitative Analysis* **45**(4): 1077–1110.

Perold, A. F. and Jr. Salomon, R. S. (1991). The right amount of assets under management, *Financial Analysts Journal* **47**(3): 31–39.

Petajisto, A. (2009). Why do demand curves for stocks slope down?, *Journal of Financial and Quantitative Analysis* **44**(5): 1013–1044.

Petersen, M. A. (2009). Estimating standard errors in finance panel data sets: Comparing approaches, *Review of Financial Studies* **22**(1): 435 –480.

Phillips, G. M. and Zhdanov, A. (2013). R&d and the incentives from merger and acquisition activity, *Review of Financial Studies* **26**(1): 34 –78.

Polk, C. K. and Sapienza, P. (2002). The real effects of investor sentiment, SSRN eLibrary .

Pratt, J. W. (1964). Risk aversion in the small and in the large, *Econometrica* **32**(1/2): 122–136.

Rabin, M. (2002). Inference by believers in the law of small numbers, *The Quarterly Journal of Economics* **117**(3): 775 –816.

Rabin, M. and Vayanos, D. (2010). The gambler's and hot-hand fallacies: Theory and applications, *The Review of Economic Studies* **77**(2): 730–778.

Radin, R. F. and Stevenson, W. B. (2006). Comparing mutual fund governance and corporate governance, Corporate Governance: *An International Review* **14**(5): 367–376.

Rajan, R. G. and Zingales, L. (1995). What do we know about capital structure? Some evidence from international data, *The Journal of Finance* **50**(5): 1421– 1460.

Rakowski, D. and Wang, X. (2009). The dynamics of short-term mutual fund flows and returns: A time-series and cross-sectional investigation, *Journal of Banking & Finance* **33**(11): 2102–2109.

Ranaldo, A. (2004). Order aggressiveness in limit order book markets, *Journal of Financial Markets* **7**(1): 53–74.

Reinganum, M. R. (1990). Market microstructure and asset pricing: An empirical investigation of NYSE and NASDAQ securities, *Journal of Financial Economics* **28**(12): 127–147.

Richards, A. (2005). Big fish in small ponds: The trading behavior and price impact of foreign investors in Asian emerging equity markets, *Journal of Financial and Quantitative Analysis* **40**(1): 1–27.

Ritter, J. R. and Welch, I. (2002). A review of IPO activity, pricing, and allocations, *The Journal of Finance* **57**(4): 1795–1828.

Roll, R. (1984). A simple implicit measure of the effective bid-ask spread in an efficient market, *The Journal of Finance* **39**(4): 1127–1139.

Romer, D. (1993). Rational asset-price movements without news, *American Economic Review* **83**(5): 1112–1130.

Roşu, I. (2009). A dynamic model of the limit order book, *Review of Financial Studies* **22**(11): 4601–4641.

Roşu, I. (2010). Liquidity and information in order driven markets, SSRN eLibrary .

Rouwenhorst, K. G. (1998). International momentum strategies, *The Journal of Finance* **53**(1): 267–284.

Rouwenhorst, K. G. (1999). Local return factors and turnover in emerging stock markets, *The Journal of Finance* **54**(4): 1439–1464.

Rudd, A. (1980). Optimal selection of passive portfolios, *Financial Management* **9**(1): 57–66.

Sadka, R. (2006). Momentum and post-earnings-announcement drift anomalies: The role of liquidity risk, *Journal of Financial Economics* **80**(2): 309–349.

Safieddine, A. and Jr. Wilhelm, W. J. (1996). An empirical investigation of short-selling activity prior to seasoned equity offerings, *The Journal of Finance* **51**(2): 729–749.

Salop, S. and Stiglitz, J. (1977). Bargains and ripoffs: A model of monopolistically competitive price dispersion, *The Review of Economic Studies* **44**(3): 493–510.

Sandroni, A. (2000). Do markets favor agents able to make accurate predictions?, *Econometrica* **68**(6): 1303–1341.

Sapp, T. and Tiwari, A. (2004). Does stock return momentum explain the "smart money" effect?, *The Journal of Finance* **59**(6): 2605–2622.

Scharfstein, D. S. and Stein, J. C. (1990). Herd behavior and investment, *American Economic Review* **80**(3): 465–479.

Scheinkman, J. A. and Xiong, W. (2003). Overconfidence and speculative bubbles, *Journal of Political Economy* **111**(6): 1183–1220.

Schneider, J. (2009). A rational expectations equilibrium with informative trading volume, *The Journal of Finance* (6): 2783–2805.

Schultz, P. (2003). Who makes markets, *Journal of Financial Markets* **6**(1): 49– 72.

Seasholes, M. S. and Zhu, N. (2010). Individual investors and local bias, *The Journal of Finance* **65**(5): 1987–2010.

Senchack, A. J. J. and Starks, L. T. (1993). Short-sale restrictions and market reaction to short-interest announcements, *Journal of Financial and Quantitative Analysis* **28**(2): 177–194.

Seru, A., Shumway, T. and Stoffman, N. (2010). Learning by trading, *Review of Financial Studies* **23**(2): 705 –739.

Sharpe, W. F. (1966). Mutual fund performance, *The Journal of Business* **39**(1): 119–138.

Shefrin, H. (2005). A behavioral approach to asset pricing. Elsevier Academic Press, New York.

Shefrin, H. and Statman, M. (1985). The disposition to sell winners too early and ride losers too long: Theory and evidence, *The Journal of Finance* **40**(3): 777– 790.

Shleifer, A. and Summers, L. H. (1990). The noise trader approach to finance, *Journal of Economic Perspectives* **4**(2): 19–33.

Shleifer, A. and Vishny, R. W. (1997). The limits of arbitrage, *The Journal of Finance* **52**(1): 35–55.

Shyam-Sunder, L. and C. Myers, S. (1999). Testing static tradeoff against pecking order models of capital structure, *Journal of Financial Economics* **51**(2): 219–244.

Sias, R. W. (2004). Institutional herding, *Review of Financial Studies* **17**(1): 165 –206.

Sias, R. W. and Starks, L. T. (1997). Return autocorrelation and institutional investors, *Journal of Financial Economics* **46**(1): 103–131.

Sias, R. W., Starks, L. T. and Titman, S. (2006). Changes in institutional ownership and stock returns: Assessment and methodology, *The Journal of Business* **79**(6): 2869–2910.

Silber, W. L. (1991). Discounts on restricted stock: The impact of illiquidity on stock prices, *Financial Analysts Journal* **47**(4): 60–64.

Simaan, Y., Weaver, D. G. and Whitcomb, D. K. (2003). Market maker quotation behavior and pretrade transparency, *The Journal of Finance* **58**(3): 1247– 1268.

Sirri, E. R. and Tufano, P. (1998). Costly search and mutual fund flows, *The Journal of Finance* **53**(5): 1589–1622.

Sorensen, E. H., Miller, K. L. and Samak, V. (1998). Allocating between active and passive management, *Financial Analysts Journal* **54**(5): 18–31.

Spiess, D. K. and Affleck-Graves, J. (1995). Underperformance in long-run stock returns following seasoned equity offerings, *Journal of Financial Economics* **38**(3): 243–267.

Starks, L. T. (1987). Performance incentive fees: An agency theoretic approach, *Journal of Financial and Quantitative Analysis* **22**(1): 17–32.

Stoll, H. R. (1989). Inferring the components of the bid-ask spread: Theory and empirical tests, *The Journal of Finance* **44**(1): 115–134.

Strahilevitz, M. A., Odean, T. and Barber, B. M. (2011). Once burned, twice shy: How naive learning, counterfactuals, and regret affect the repurchase of stocks previously sold, *Journal of Marketing Research* **48**: S102–S120.

Strebulaev, I. A. (2007). Do tests of capital structure theory mean what they say?, *The Journal of Finance* **62**(4): 1747–1787.

Stulz, R. M. (1981a). A model of international asset pricing, *Journal of Financial Economics* **9**(4): 383–406.

Stulz, R. M. (1981b). On the effects of barriers to international investment, *The Journal of Finance* **36**(4): 923–934.

Stulz, R. M. (2009). Securities laws, disclosure, and national capital markets in the age of financial globalization, *Journal of Accounting Research* **47**(2): 349–390.

Subrahmanyam, A. (1991). A theory of trading in stock index futures, *Review of Financial Studies* **4**(1): 17–51.

Subrahmanyam, A. and Titman, S. (1999). The going-public decision and the development of financial markets, *The Journal of Finance* **54**(3): 1045–1082.

Sun, Z., Wang, A. and Zheng, L. (2012). The road less traveled: Strategy distinctiveness and hedge fund performance, *Review of Financial Studies* **25**(1): 96 –143.

Suominen, M. (2001). Trading volume and information revelation in stock markets, *Journal of Financial and Quantitative Analysis* **36**(4): 545–565.

Taylor, L. A. (2010). Why are CEOs rarely fired? Evidence from structural estimation, *The Journal of Finance* **65**(6): 2051–2087.

Tesar, L. L. and Werner, I. M. (1995). Home bias and high turnover, *Journal of International Money and Finance* **14**(4): 467–492.

Tetlock, P. C. (2010). Does public financial news resolve asymmetric information?, *Review of Financial Studies* **23**(9): 3520 –3557.

Thaler, R. H. and Johnson, E. J. (1990). Gambling with the house money and trying to break even: The effects of prior outcomes on risky choice, *Management Science* **36**(6): 643–660.

Tirole, J. (2011). Illiquidity and all its friends, *Journal of Economic Literature* **49**(2): 287–325.

Titman, S., Wei, K. C. J. and Xie, F. (2004). Capital investments and stock returns, *Journal of Financial and Quantitative Analysis* **39**(4): 677–700.

Titman, S. and Wessels, R. (1988). The determinants of capital structure choice, *The Journal of Finance* **43**(1): 1–19.

Tookes, H. E. (2008). Information, trading, and product market interactions: Cross-sectional implications of informed trading, *The Journal of Finance* **63**(1): 379–413.

Tufano, P. and Sevick, M. (1997). Board structure and fee-setting in the U.S. mutual fund industry, *Journal of Financial Economics* **46**(3): 321–355.

Tversky, A. and Kahneman, D. (1971). Belief in the law of small numbers, *Psychological Bulletin* **76**(2): 105–110.

van Bommel, J. (2003). Rumors, *The Journal of Finance* **58**(4): 1499–1520.

Vissing-Jorgensen, A. (2003). Perspectives on behavioral finance: Does "irrationality" disappear with wealth? Evidence from expectations and actions, NBER Macroeconomics Annual 18: 139–194.

Vives, X. (2008). Information and learning in markets: The impact of market microstructure Princeton University Press, Princeton.

Wachter, J. A. (2010). Asset allocation, *Annual Review of Financial Economics* **2**(1): 175–206.

Wagner, W. (2011). Systemic liquidation risk and the diversity-diversification trade-off, *The Journal of Finance* **66**(4): 1141–1175.

Wagner, W. H. and Zipkin, C. A. (1978). Can inventory index funds improve active equity performance?, *Financial Analysts Journal* **34**(3): 34–76.

Wahal, S. (1997). Entry, exit, market makers, and the bid-ask spread, *Review of Financial Studies* **10**(3): 871 –901.

Wang, F. A. (2001). Overconfidence, investor sentiment, and evolution, *Journal of Financial Intermediation* 10(2): 138–170.

Wang, J. (1993). A model of intertemporal asset prices under asymmetric information, *The Review of Economic Studies* **60**(2): 249–282.

Welch, I. (2004). Capital structure and stock returns, *Journal of Political Economy* **112**(1): 106–132.

Wermers, R. (1999). Mutual fund herding and the impact on stock prices, *The Journal of Finance* **54**(2): 581–622.

Wermers, R. (2000). Mutual fund performance: An empirical decomposition into stock-picking talent, style, transactions costs, and expenses, *The Journal of Finance* **55**(4): 1655–1703.

Wermers, R. (2006). Performance evaluation with portfolio holdings information, *The North American Journal of Economics and Finance* **17**(2): 207–230.

Wilcox, R. T. (2003). Bargain hunting or star gazing? investors' preferences for stock mutual funds, *The Journal of Business* **76**(4): 645–663.

Wolf, J. (1990). Calendar spreads for enhanced index fund returns, *Financial Analysts Journal* **46**(1): 66–79.

Wruck, K. H. (1989). Equity ownership concentration and firm value : Evidence from private equity financings, *Journal of Financial Economics* **23**(1): 3–28.

Wruck, K. H. and Wu, Y. (2009). Relationships, corporate governance, and performance: Evidence from private placements of common stock, *Journal of Corporate Finance* **15**(1): 30–47.

Wylie, S. (2005). Fund manager herding: A test of the accuracy of empirical results using U.K. data, *The Journal of Business* **78**(1): 381–403. Yeo, W. Y. (2006). Persistence in limit order flow, SSRN eLibrary .

Zhao, X. (2004). Why are some mutual funds closed to new investors?, *Journal of Banking & Finance* **28**(8): 1867–1887.

Zheng, L. (1999). Is money smart? a study of mutual fund investors' fund selection ability, *The Journal of Finance* **54**(3): 901–933.

Zwiebel, J. (1995). Corporate conservatism and relative compensation, *Journal of Political Economy* **103**(1): 1–25.